NICK

THE JOURNEY OF A LIFETIME

Christine Schimpf

A NOVEL

T0204800

INSPIRED BY TRUE EVENTS

Thank you supporting Wisconsin
writers. Enjoy the journey
of Nick's lifetime.

Christine Schimpf

ISBN-13:978-1468164268
ISBN-1468164260

For the love of my life, Ernie

Acknowledgments

First, I extend immense gratitude to my writing colleagues and to our instructor, Gail; to my editors: Sharon, Trish, and Karen; and to the Emerging Authors group. I am the one truly blessed to have found all of you.

Many others have helped me along the way including Nick's two daughters Leni (Magdalena/Helen) Schimpf and Kati (Katarina) Mueller along with their husbands Nikolaus Schimpf and Jacob Mueller. Thank you for filling in the gaps and explaining your perspective. Without your help, the edges would have remained rough and the associations weak.

Most important, I want to acknowledge my husband, Ernie, who has encouraged me to write for more than twenty years. I thank my children, who not only reassured me, but believed in my ability to turn my dream into reality.

And last but not least, if my gratitude could extend into the next world, let it reach Nick. I hope that he is smiling now and is proud of what I have produced of his life's journey. Thank you for sharing with me your pure, unabridged insight and for the privilege you gave me to write your story.

PREFACE

I remember the first time I met Nicholas Russ. The German family I was blessed to marry into called him *Ota,* an endearing nickname for grandfather. When asked to write *Ota's* story, I immediately felt challenged yet invigorated, despite the enormity of the task.ᵌ I encouraged *Ota* to simply share with me the stories of his life. Some memories flooded his mind and the words came easily while others were caught up in the language barrier and my own inability to understand life outside of America.

He waits for me now sitting on a picnic table at his home. Like a fat old owl he holds the secrets of the past. I will record these visits to weave a story of his life's journey. He smiles as I approach him. His amber-colored glasses and white cap protect his eyes from the bright sun. I notice how easily his small frame rises and falls with each breath. His arms rest quietly at his sides as he repeatedly drums his fingers across the table.

PROLOGUE

In the 1800s, the Empress of the Austro-Hungarian Empire encouraged ethnic Germans to migrate to the newly acquired region along the Danube River. These emigrants became known as Donauschwabians and from here Nick's roots are traced. When Marshal Josip Broz Tito, a communist leader, gained strength in Yugoslavia during World War II, the Donauschwabians were forced to flee their homeland in order to save their lives or suffer the persecution of imprisonment or death.

CALMA

As in America, the 1920s were lucrative years for the residents of Calma. Nick's birthplace is a small, farming community near the Danube and Tisa Rivers in the Austro-Hungarian Empire. The village of Calma was comprised predominantly of Eastern Orthodox Serbians and German Catholics with a minority of Hungarians and Croatians. Two churches, Holy Wendelin Catholic Church and the Eastern Orthodox Church, flanked its borders.

In 1918, Nick's birthplace underwent a name change as the result of WWI and the Treaty of Versailles from the Austro-Hungarian Empire to the Kingdom of the Serbs, Croats, and Slovenes. In 1929, the kingdom was renamed Yugoslavia. Today, it is the independent state of Serbia.

Most of the villagers were considered Calma's working class poor. For example, while the wealthy could afford "real" brick for their homes, most of the farmers created an imitation brick made of mud which was high in clay and mixed with the wheat and rye husks. The mud was shaped into the identical shape of the authentic brick and set aside to dry in the sun. The bricks were then laid one on top of another and mortared together with the same muddy mixture. Roof tile was made from the same material but fired in a kiln, turning it a rich, brick red.

Occupations were usually passed down from previous generations. Typically, most young men followed the footsteps of their fathers and became farmers. This central region was made up of rich soil perfect for growing wheat, corn, and hay or raising cattle, chickens, and pigs. The area was also known for its mineral water, goose down, and duck feathers.

The region was so fertile that it produced an abundance of strawberries, cherries, raspberries, peaches, apricots, blackberries and melons in the spring and summer. When fall arrived, so did the grapes, apples, pears and plums.

Cobblestone roads were built to accommodate the wheat-filled wagons returning home with their harvest. During the fall of the year, one of the farmers would make his way visiting neighbors with a threshing machine, harvesting the wheat. Since currency was scarce, many villagers paid for his service by offering a percentage of their bound stacks for payment. This bartering was an accepted way of life and was repeated for many other goods and services throughout the community.

While most young men chose farming the land there were others who inherited milking cow farms which produced a similar living. Each morning the herd would be guided through the village to the grazing fields. The herders would use sticks and dogs to keep the herd moving in the right path. After grazing, the cows would be milked by hand. The milk was stored in large metal containers which were then hauled off for deliveries among the residents and businesses.

In order to build his family a nice home, *Ota's* father found work in America laboring in the steel factories. The pay was good, but the price was long-term absence from his family. Typically, he would be gone for years at a time, sending money home so his family was well taken care of. Since *Ota* loved the feel and smell of wood, his father secured an apprenticeship for him with his Uncle Philip, who worked as a master carpenter and had his own shop in Calma.

In 1924, at the age of 12, right after finishing primary school, *Ota* began a three-year carpentry apprenticeship under the supervision of Uncle Philip. Ota's father provided a half a pig and one meter of flour for food and lodging and it is a few years after this time period, when this story begins.

Chapter One

The music inside the *gasthaus* thumped strongly and mingled with the chatter, laughter, and gaiety from within. Nick moved quickly down the cobblestone street toward the gates that would let him in. He was young, strong, and confident. Working as an apprentice allowed the coins in his pocket to jingle. He felt good. He earned this.

He narrowed his eyes and squinted through the wooden planks at the locked gate. A feeling of isolation settled in as he gazed at the party he so much wanted to join. In order to get in, he knew he would have to pay the price. Even though he wasn't quite old enough, he knew the older boys who guarded the gate would let him in for the price of a few wine tokens.

"Hey Russ," sneered Jacob, one of the older boys, "where do you think you're going?"

Nick snapped his head in Jacob's direction, "Where do you think?" he asked, "like everybody else, I want to go in."

"Oh, yeah, well, you're going to have to pay up then." Jacob thrust his sweaty palm toward Nick for payment.

Nick placed three wine tokens that he had

managed to pilfer at his Uncle Philip's, into Jacob's fleshy open hand. He pushed the entrance gate open, and let himself in.

"Thanks party boy," Jacob sneered, "see you next time." A loud roar of laughter broke out among the older boys.

Nick turned toward the light that reflected in the shiny brass instruments piping out the familiar tunes. The dry, musty scent of burning wood chips for the *spanferkel* planned for later made his mouth water. The afternoon was warm. A light, wispy breeze swept across the crowd, and caused welcomed sighs of relief from the exhausted dancers.

Nick loved the dances held at the local *gasthaus* and tried not to miss many, even if it meant a day's journey from his job in the neighboring village. The dances were a part of a pre-Lenten celebration in the spring and ended during harvest season. The afternoon dances brought the village Germans together in a pleasant social setting. Nick was surrounded by laughing, dancing villagers, yet he moved swiftly through the crowd. He smiled at some, nodded at others, and made his way toward his favorite girl.

Standing near her friends, Theresa smiled as she thought of Nick. She hoped he would make it to the dance today, but so far, she hadn't seen him. She let her mind wander a bit and remembered the first time she had met Nick. It was through the unintentional efforts of her stepbrother, Joe. He and Nick were best friends, and they spent a lot of time together. When Nick's visits became more and more frequent, she realized he had affection for her, and she for him and that's where it all started.

Nick and Theresa's relationship grew beneath the watchful eyes of everyone around them, despite the fact that Theresa's stepfather had promised her hand in marriage to someone else. Theresa liked Nick right from the start. He talked a lot and acted like he had plans for the future, plans she so much wanted to be a part of. Deep down, Theresa knew Nick felt the same way about her as she did of him. He loved to make her laugh. She could see it in his eyes when they lit up when he told his stories. She felt safe near Nick, although Nick was no saint – Theresa knew that much from experience. Before they became serious, she had caught Nick and Joe sneaking out to smoke cigarettes behind the barn. She giggled to herself recalling the memory and how angry Joe had gotten when Nick decided to invite Theresa and her stepsister along.

"What do we need to bring the girls along for, Nick?" asked Joe.

"Think about it, would you, Joe? If we take them with us, and make them smoke too, we're in the clear. They can't turn us in because they're as guilty as we are."

Joe smiled. *That Nick,* he thought, *always thinking.*

Theresa started to fidget, shuffling her feet back and forth. *Where is he?* She asked herself. *Shouldn't he be here by now?* Then she heard his voice behind her.

"How about a dance, Theresa?" Nick stammered.

Theresa slowly turned from her friends and faced Nick. Her eyes immediately smiled. Although Theresa's parents forbade her to date Nick because a marriage was being arranged for her with her stepfather's nephew, the couple had found stolen moments to be together, and their feelings for each other had grown into love.

"I'd love to dance with you, Nick," Theresa replied eagerly.

As Theresa moved toward Nick, he noticed how beautiful she was that day. The dress she was wearing was one of his favorites. He secretly hoped she had picked it out just for him. Nick and Theresa slipped away from their friends and walked toward the other dancers. Nick felt his heart pounding, his brow light with perspiration, and hands suddenly clammy. When they reached the dance floor, Nick held out his hand and Theresa easily slipped into his arms. She felt so right, so perfect. He breathed in her scent. Almost giddy, he led her in dance around the floor.

"Look at the lovebirds," someone said behind them. Nick and Theresa did not respond to the comment. At that moment, they had forgotten everyone else. Instead, they began to circle the floor, in their familiar way, glancing at each other, faces flushed, and smiles bright.

As they slowly made their way around the dance floor, Nick silently compared his life to that of Theresa's. He knew her stepfather had a habit of drinking too much schnapps every night, and now Nick had heard rumors of him marrying Theresa off to a butcher a few villages away. Nick could feel the anger rise from his belly as his thoughts chased him step for step as he continued to glide across the floor. The music rose and fell, along with his emotions. He knew something had to change before it was too late, and he'd lose her forever. As the music began its descent, Nick's arms curled around Theresa's waist. He smiled into her pretty face and warm brown eyes. Her fingers gently stroked the side of his face. At that moment, he knew he didn't want to face a day without her in his life. He knew what had to be done. He wanted to take care of Theresa, forever.

Chapter Two

It was a cold January night but the small brick home stood its ground. The winter wind howled as it slapped up against the house, curled around the chimney, and swept straight down into the kitchen, almost extinguishing the fire in the cornstalk burner. Theresa shuddered as she worked quickly washing the kitchen table, rinsing her dishrag, and returning to the remaining dishes. Her stepfather and his nephew Michael spoke quietly in the next room. Theresa pressed her ear against the wall nearest the door trying to hear something from the conversation, yet fearing what the two men discussed. She heard the schnapps bottle landing on the nearby table with a loud *thump!* She took a few steps toward the open doorway and inched her eye beyond the doorframe, just enough to get a glimpse.

"So, it is set then," Michael said with a snort. Large, thick hands, weathered from a day's work, clapped together as he faced Theresa's stepfather. Although several teeth were missing in his lower jaw, Michael smiled widely, as he sucked in gulps of air. He ran his fingers through his hair, more out of habit than need. Ruddy cheeks and a strong, thick neck led to a stout frame with solid, large feet.

"Yes, it is a match," replied Theresa's stepfather.

"You and Theresa will be wed. We leave in the morning."

Theresa heard two glasses clinking together, sealing their agreement. Michael stomped his foot while extending his right hand. The two men grasped each other's hands and shook fiercely, with a fire of excitement in their eyes.

A soft knock on the kitchen back door broke the scene and caused Theresa to jump half a step. Theresa's best friend, Hilde, pressed her nose against the cold window pane and waited patiently on the stoop. Theresa quickly unlatched the door, swung it open, and hurried her friend inside.

"Hilde," Theresa blurted, "I'm so glad you are here. My stepfather and Michael are making arrangements for my wedding to Michael! I am to leave in the morning with him! What am I to do?"

"Why don't you try to talk with your stepfather? Just tell him you love Nick."

"He told me I will be well taken care of as a butcher's wife; that I will learn to love Michael in time! He wants me to forget about Nick because he has no money, not like Michael!"

Hilde could see the pain Theresa felt as she wrung her hands over and over and stared out the kitchen window. She bent over the sink and began to sob. Hilde moved slowly across the kitchen toward Theresa in small, calculated steps, placed her coat over a chair, and removed her hat. She could hear the voices from the next room getting louder and more jovial. She stopped her pacing, faced Theresa, and opened her arms for her.

"You must help me, Hilde," Theresa whispered,

as she laid her head on Hilde's shoulder. "You must find Nick. He should be on his way over here. I'm afraid, Hilde, and Nick ... Nick will know what to do."

"Yes, okay," Hilde whispered in Theresa's ear, "Everything will be all right, Theresa, please don't worry."

With a frightened look, Theresa took a step back, peering into the eyes of her best friend, shook her head back and forth slowly, as her eyes filled with tears.

Chapter Three

Nick turned up his collar against the biting wind, shoved his hands deep into his pockets, and continued on his way down the quiet street in Calma. He heard a dog howling in the distance and picked up his pace. He had planned on spending another evening at Theresa's visiting with her and her stepbrother, Joe. He loved spending time with Theresa, and under the guise of his friendship with Joe, things could not have worked out more perfectly. Four years had passed since he first noticed Theresa. Living three doors away from each other made it difficult not to notice her. Nick was immediately drawn to her beauty, but it was her spirit that kept him guessing. She spoke her mind, and he liked that.

Nick understood why Theresa's parents wanted Michael for her husband instead of him. Michael had an established business as a butcher and meat was a high commodity. Most village residents ate meat once a week and Theresa, and her family, would never know hunger if the marriage went through as planned. But Nick was making progress in his own line of work as a cabinet maker. Now with his apprenticeship behind him, he was working toward earning hours in his Journeymen's Ledger.

According to the law, an apprentice had to track project hours in a Journeymen's Ledger along with the consent of a master carpenter. When the quota of hours was accumulated, the apprentice would complete a written examination and build a project. Only then would a Master's Card be earned.

From 1927 to 1931, Nick worked toward earning as many hours as possible and seeing Theresa as much as possible too. He had traveled to Backa and Streslovonia, nearly 100 kilometers away, to get as many hours as he could building bedroom furniture, kitchen tables, chairs, dressers and picture frames but he always returned to Calma and his Theresa who was waiting for him. Once he satisfied the hour requirement, he would take an examination, build his project, and earn his Master's Card. Then he'd be free to open his own shop. He wanted this dream to come true more than anything else he had ever wanted before but not more than wanting Theresa at his side, as his wife. Only then, would his dream be complete and his life perfect.

The village of Calma looked beautiful to Nick as the new fallen snow swirled around him. He felt good about his life and what it held for him and Theresa. Soon, he would be finished accumulating hours in his Journeymen's Ledger and he would take the examination for his Master's Card and build his project. He could hardly wait. Lost in his own thoughts, Nick was suddenly interrupted by the sound of someone running toward him. He forced his eyes to focus into the blackness ahead of him but the snow whipped at his eyes causing a sting, his feet fell to a slow pace, ears perked and alert. *Could that be ... Hilde?* Whoever it was, she was headed right toward him, clearly out of breath, with a look of panic. *This can't be good.* Nick stopped abruptly waiting to confirm his suspicion until Hilde was upon him.

"What is it, Hilde? Why are you running like this?"

"Nick, please ... come quickly... Theresa..."

When Nick heard Theresa's name mentioned, his heart began beating as if it would jump out of his chest. He could feel his hands ball up into fists but he knew he had to try to remain calm to hear what Hilde had to tell him.

"Theresa! What about Theresa, is she all right?"

Hilde bent over gasping in big gulps of air. She grabbed Nick's coat sleeve to steady herself, "Her stepfather and his nephew," she wheezed, "they are talking about the marriage again. They are leaving tomorrow."

Nick immediately knew what Hilde was trying to tell him. Something inside of him clicked. A feeling of calm overtook him, his fists unclenched, and he wasn't afraid anymore. He wasn't even angry. Instead, he felt strong. He felt like a man ready to make his move.

"Hilde, now listen to me," Nick instructed, "Go back to Theresa. Tell her to pack her things, and I will come for her tonight."

"*Ja*, Nick, I will." As Hilde faded into the darkness, Nick's parting words followed her, "Tell her to keep watch by the small window."

Nick moved quickly with purpose to his step. His feet landed firmly on the street, arms pumping back and forth to help him pick up speed. The wind whipped at his face causing a bite, but unlike earlier, he ignored the weather's fury and kept up his rapid pace. He was headed in the direction of his sister Helen's house, just across town. The four of them, Nick, Theresa, Helen and Josef, had a plan in place for months just in case something like this were to happen. Now it was time to put that plan into action.

Nick turned down the narrow street and remembered a night not too long ago, at Theresa's, when he thought his feelings for Theresa were finally recognized by her mother, Mrs. Helleis. Finally, he hoped that she was actually changing her mind and would allow him to marry Theresa. It was during corn harvest; Nick had come over to see Joe with intentions of spending time with Theresa. The family was stuffing shucked corn husks into large sheets that had been sewn together to make comforters. When they were finished for the night, Mrs. Helleis told the children to carry the comforters up to the attic for storage.

"Are you planning to help, Nick, or just sit there gazing at my Theresa?"

"Oh, yes, yes," Nick stuttered, clumsily getting to his feet, thankful to do something to hide his reddened cheeks.

"What if I said to you, if you don't help carry the comforters up, I won't allow you to marry my Theresa?" She laughed heartily, turned her back to him, and returned to the task at hand.

Nick quickly scooped up as many comforters as he could hold. Hoping not to stumble, he clumsily made his way up the attic stairs. "Oh! No, no, Mrs. Helleis, I can carry ALL the comforters up!"

Yet, soon after that incident, everyone returned

back to the same old notion of Theresa marrying Michael. *It was never a secret about how I felt about her,* Nick thought as he turned the corner and entered his sister's yard. He sprinted up the steps to the front door, rapped three times hard. The door swung open and the warm glow from the room inside spilled out onto the landing, illuminating Nick's face.

"Nick!" shouted his brother-in-law, Josef, "Come on in."

Chapter Four

Theresa silently waited near the window. She pressed her nose against the cold glass while tightening her grip on the bundled sheet holding her belongings. She lifted the edge of the worn fabric to her lips and nervously began biting at the frayed edges.

"Hurry, Nick, hurry, hurry, hurry," she whispered. But there was no reply. The darkness surrounded her. She was alone and frightened, afraid of being found out and their plan spoiled. Everyone was sleeping in the house except Theresa. Just down the hall, Theresa could hear Michael's snoring. He had enjoyed supper with them and had turned in early. Theresa was expected to leave Calma forever, marry Michael, and never look back. This was the reason she was waiting at the window, her only escape.

When Hilde had returned earlier that evening, she had given Theresa explicit instructions from Nick. Theresa should be ready and waiting. She had to use the window because it was the quietest escape route from the house. She couldn't risk opening the front door with all of its squeaks and groans. Surely, doing that would wake someone. Theresa would have loved for Hilde to stay with her and wait for Nick and Josef's arrival but it was too dangerous. The house had to remain as quiet as possible. Theresa was on her own.

Theresa stared out the window, seeing movement in the distance. Her breath caught in her throat at the sight of Nick walking alongside Josef.

"Just as we planned," Theresa murmured, a smile slowly made its way across her small face.

Soon, both men were standing below her window, beckoning her to come down.

Nick stood firmly with his feet planted and both arms outstretched to help her. His smile lit up the night. Josef was nearby, watching and waiting for any sign of movement from within the house.

Slowly, Theresa opened the window, hoping to avoid making a sound. She lifted up her knapsack of belongings and dropped it into the waiting arms of Josef.

"Got it," he mouthed back to her.

Then she boosted herself up onto the sill. Small slivers of wood burrowed their way into her palms. She flinched, more annoyed with herself for not thinking to protect her hands, and forced one leg up, and then the other, over the window's ledge. Quickly, she flipped over onto her stomach, forcing her feet into the small notches on the side of the house. She inched herself down along the edge of the sill hoping the descent was not high enough to cause injury should she fall yet dismissing the fear knowing that Nick would be there to catch her if she did. Down, down, down as far as she could go. Finally, she counted, *one, two, three* and let go completely, falling backwards and into the arms of Nick.

"There you go my darling," Nick whispered into her ear.

Theresa turned and looked up in the eyes of her

true intended, a bit stunned at her sudden bolt of courage.

"What is this?" she asked, lifting a bottle of wine sticking out of Nick's coat pocket.

Nick winked his reply, "It is for us, Theresa, for later."

Chapter Five

They had been walking only a short while when Nick realized Theresa had become quiet.

"Cold, Theresa?" Nick asked when he noticed she seemed a bit melancholy.

"No, Nick, I'm warm now," she said smiling and turning back toward him. "Everything's alright."

Josef shook his head. Still holding Theresa's knapsack, he smiled at the couple and pushed on.

The two men talked easily as they made their way across town, the threat of being found out over, the burden of reaching Theresa in time, now lifted. As they turned the last corner, Nick noticed the lamp softly illuminating the window and felt enormous gratitude for Helen's thoughtfulness. He reached over and pulled Theresa closer, tucking her snugly under his arm.

Once inside, Helen embraced Theresa with all the excitement of a child seeing Saint Nicholas. A thin, frail woman, Helen was known in the family as kind and gentle, with a soft heart. She kissed Theresa on the cheek and whispered privately to her, "I'm sorry it's come to this for you, Theresa, but I know my brother loves you dearly. Real love finds a way to win out in the end."

Their eyes met and twinkled, smiles reflecting each other's eagerness for the future.

"*Ja,* I guess it does, Helen," Theresa replied. "Nick got there just in time. My parents wanted me to marry Michael. We were intending on leaving first thing in the morning!"

"That was exactly what we were afraid of happening," Helen sighed.

Theresa shook her head from side to side, still shaken by the night's events.

"Now, please, sit down all of you," Helen ordered trying to calm the group, "I've got a pot of coffee brewing and some fresh plum *kipfel* I just baked this morning." As Helen turned and left the room, her fingers gently brushed Josef's shoulder, and she smiled. Josef acted on the silent cue from his wife and invited Nick and Theresa to the nearby sofa.

Moments later, Helen was carrying four steaming cups of coffee placed on a wooden serving platter Nick had made for her years ago.

"Well, where do we go from here?" Helen asked as she served each family member their portion of coffee and *kipfel*. Her eyes quickly darted from Nick to Theresa, her lips falling silent for their reply. The wind picked up outside causing the shutters to bang against the house. Josef shot up out of his chair, startled, and pulled the soft draperies across the two windows, closing out all interference.

"Tonight, we stay put, just as we planned," Nick said. "I expect Theresa's family to be pretty upset when they find out that she is gone, and I'm sure this is the first place they'll come looking."

"Are you concerned about that, Nick?" Josef asked.

"Well, *ja*," Nick replied. "Our problem now is that Theresa is only 17 and her mother has refused to sign the consent allowing her to marry me."

"It just means you have to wait it out, Nick," Helen replied in a soothing voice.

Nick wrung his hands and felt agitated. He wasn't sure how to handle an emotional outburst from Theresa's mother once she realized Theresa had run off with him.

"Listen, Nick," Josef interrupted his thoughts. "Tonight you are here and you are safe, and whatever happens, we'll handle it together, as a family."

"Couples fall in love. Couples run off and elope. It happens," Helen added with a smile.

"It happens," Nick repeated, still unconvinced of the certainty his sister apparently felt. The four finished up their conversation and Nick found himself calming down and enjoying the evening the more they discussed how they would handle different scenarios.

"Well, it's getting quite late," Helen said after a few hours had passed. "I've made up the spare room for you both. Tomorrow, we'll talk about where to go from here. Try to get some rest."

"Thank you, Helen." Nick reached out to give his sister a hug. "We couldn't have done this without your help."

As the four parted for the evening, Nick suddenly realized he and Theresa would actually be spending their first night together. As he picked up his jacket off the chair, he remembered the bottle of wine still sitting in his coat pocket. He felt a bit anxious. He squeezed his eyes shut and swallowed thickly trying to regain his confidence as they made their way to their room.

"Well, Theresa, any regrets?" Nick reached out for her with a tight smile after he softly closed their bedroom door. The room looked lovely. A soft multicolored quilt was spread across the bed, flanked by two overstuffed pillows in embroidered pillowcases. A thick feather comforter was folded neatly at the foot. A small lamp, dimly lit, was burning on the nightstand, cascading a shadowy pattern throughout the room. He could feel a slight tremor throughout his body and prayed that she wasn't thinking twice about marrying him.

"Regrets, Nick? Absolutely not," Theresa whispered. She placed her clothes bundle on the chair nearby, began unbuttoning her sweater, and walked straight toward him.

With trembling fingers, Nick reached out for her, closing the space between them, and the two embraced in the quiet of the night.

Tick, tick, tick, tick, the sound of the clock sitting on the nightstand was driving Nick right out of his mind! He had been awake for hours now – wondering, worrying, thinking, and planning. He placed both palms at his temples and pushed his head like a nut in a vise. A light perspiration laced his brow. He turned over on his side, hoping not to stir Theresa. She was sleeping so soundly, such innocence. What was he going to do if Theresa's mother and stepdad came over tomorrow looking for her? Harsh words would be exchanged. Feelings would be high. More importantly, they might take her from him. He might lose her forever. She was underage. A run-a-way! Nick turned over onto his back and stared into the blackness. The only answer he could come up with was to return to the safe haven of his parents' home. After all, it was *tradition* to live with your parents. Nick drew in a ragged breath and slowly exhaled. He already felt better with his decision, and he was certain that Theresa would agree. He let his body sink into the soft mattress, pulling the comforter around him. Turning toward her, he slipped an arm around her small waist, and drifted off to sleep.

Chapter Six

Despite Nick's apprehension, the next several months moved by surprisingly without conflict and without a visit from Theresa's mother or stepdad. In fact, there was absolutely no contact whatsoever. *It's one way to punish someone*, Nick thought, *just cut them off completely*. Theresa and Nick lived comfortably with Nick's parents just as Nick suspected they would. On their wedding day, November 23, 1930, they both received a surprise they didn't expect – Theresa's parents refused to attend the ceremony. Although she tried to hide it, Nick knew their decision not to attend affected her deeply. Shortly after the wedding, for reasons unknown to Nick and Theresa, her parents moved to Slankament, a neighboring village about 50 kilometers away. Not a word was spoken. They simply picked up and left town. Theresa and Nick were on their own.

For Nick, the next step was to keep cataloging his hours in his Journeyman's Ledger and to get some money coming in. After all, he had a wife to support. It wouldn't be long and he would finally be able to take the examination and get his Master's Card, just a few more hours, a few more projects. He had to just hold on.

"Hey Nick," said Josef across the table one morning over coffee. "Let's open up a business. What do you do you say?"

"What do you mean? Are you thinking a partnership?"

"That's right. With my masonry skills and your cabinet building expertise, we could really build a solid business and make a good living. We both bring in business, and split the profits 50/50."

"That's something to think about," Nick said. But it didn't take Nick long to decide. He was in and he and Josef put their heads together and began building a business from the ground up. However, as months passed, tensions grew. Despite their best intentions, their family bond, and their close friendship, the two men just couldn't see eye to eye on many of the aspects of how to actually *run the business*. Nick knew things had to change. He just didn't know how or what to do.

"Rettler came in today and placed his order for a bed," Josef mentioned to Nick.

Nick could feel his stomach tighten. He had heard that the Rettlers wanted a new bed and was excited about the project coming in. He was afraid to ask, but he knew he had to.

"I hope this job pays in cash. Our revenue is down, and we really need the money."

"Well," Josef stammered, "actually, he offered to butcher some of his best chickens and when the fall wheat is in…"

"Wait a minute here." Nick interrupted Josef in midstream. "How many times are you going to pull this? We need money, Josef. Money! Not chickens, not wheat, not sausage! When are you are going to understand that?!"

"We can't expect people to give us what they don't have, Nick. These are tough times."

"Listen Josef," Nick paused a moment then continued, "This isn't for me. I'm out of this partnership. I've been thinking this over for months now and my Uncle has offered me a job where I can make steady pay, and I've … I've got to take it, Josef. This business of ours, it's tearing me apart. I hope you understand."

Josef wiped his brow with the back of his dirty hand. He looked at Nick warily and took a few steps toward him while Nick instinctively backed away, expecting the worst but unsure how to prepare. He wasn't really a fighting man, but he knew he had set off a trigger in Josef.

"Hey, hold on now, Nick," Josef said, raising both of his hands in a makeshift peace offering. "I understand. Go ahead; go back to your Uncle Phillip's. That's probably where you belong anyway."

The two men shook hands, but when their eyes met, Nick felt a shift. Something had changed, and it wasn't for the better. Nick bent over and started collecting his tools, tossing them in his toolbox. The wooden box shook with each new clank of metal against wood. He took his time placing the odds and ends that remained in some type of order, trying to make the departure a little easier. But it wasn't. A special bond was broken, a trust denied. The hours passed and he realized he simply had nothing else to do but leave. He was ready to go. He wished he could be anywhere but where he was.

"See you at Sunday supper." Nick tried to lift the mood that had crept in like fog during the night, as he took the first steps through the doorway. He dared not look back at Josef.

"Okay, Nick," Josef managed to reply.

The door slammed shut and Nick knew the partnership was dissolved.

Chapter Seven

The bad times that Josef had spoken of a few years ago, had turned into a deep economic recession. Work became scarce, men desperate. Working at Uncle Phillip's, Nick had finally managed to earn all the mandatory hours he needed for his Journeyman's Ledger. Although meager, the pay was steady. It had taken Nick years to get to this point but the recession made it tough for him and everyone else to get work. He felt ready to take the exam for his Master's Card, but the right time never seemed to come. When Theresa told him they were expecting a baby in May, he was first elated, and then worried. He did not want his young family to be a burden to his parents. So he took on as many projects as he could get, even if it meant building picture frames or traveling to another village, as long as it paid in cash. The exam could wait but the money couldn't.

Thinking of Theresa now, Nick realized how much happier and more settled she seemed since her parents moved away. In their absence, Theresa found her place in the world. He especially loved watching her care for her garden; she seemed the happiest there. And she was a blessing to his mother, helping her with the endless household chores. She was learning how to become a good "*hausfrau*" and he was proud to call her his wife.

Life was improving, slowly, until the day everything changed.

One afternoon at work, Nick was staining a cabinet he had just built, when he noticed his buddy Karl standing in the doorway. Nick dunked the large brush into the bucket of mineral spirits, pulled the rag out from his back pocket, and began wiping his hands.

"Karl, it's good to see you," Nick said, walking toward him.

"Are you ready to put in that order for the sewing table for your Mother?"

"Nick," Karl said while nodding at Uncle Phillip who was working nearby.

"No, Nick, I'm here about the news - did you hear yet?" Karl slipped a hand through his disheveled hair and took a seat near the doorway while Uncle Phillip lumbered closer.

"News?" Nick asked while bolting toward Karl thinking of Theresa. Lately, it's all he seemed to think about. The baby. The baby.

"Is it Theresa? Is she okay?"

"No, no, it's not Theresa. I'm sure she's just fine. Mom's over there today, and I'm sure you would've heard if something happened." Karl interrupted him. "It's us, Nick."

"Us? What do you mean us?"

"Our names were posted in the village square. We're headed for Karlovac, buddy, along with everybody else in our class." As Karl patted Nick on the back, it felt to Nick, like he just dropped a bomb in the room.

"Well, well, well," smirked Uncle Phillip while

working on a seed that had been caught in his tooth since lunch, "it looks like it's finally your turn, kid."

"Me?" Nick questioned, as if forgetting that every young man had to serve a six-month term in the Yugoslavia army.

"Well, we all have to go, Nick, that's the new law. We leave on May 6," Karl said with an energy Nick didn't recognize.

Nick started gathering up his coat, hat, and lunch pail, practically tripping over his own feet. "Listen, Karl, I've got to get home. I want to be the one to tell Theresa before someone else does. Uncle Phillip, I'm, I'm... heading out. I'll see you tomorrow."

"*Ja*, sure, kid."

Chapter Eight

Nick waited long after supper to break the news to his family. He wasn't looking forward to it, and he was uncertain how to handle Theresa's reaction. With less than a month until the baby's arrival, she was very emotional, sensitive, and even argumentative at times. His stomach lurched. His whole body felt jittery. *Just calm down* he said to himself, trying to regain his focus.

"Theresa, Mom, *Fater* you'd better sit down. I've got some news I need to tell you."

As the three took their favorite seats in the next room, Nick began to explain what he had learned that day, that he and several of his buddies had been conscripted into the Yugoslavia Army program and were headed for Karlovatz. Nick had gone down to the village square before heading home to make sure Karl was right. And he was. Nick saw his name in black and white, appearing larger than anyone else's name on the list. He announced the news quickly, as if he were leaving within the hour. His parents handled it better than he had expected. But Theresa was clearly upset and brought it up to him as soon as they were alone in their room.

"Nick, what does this mean? Why you? Certainly the army knows you are needed here with the baby coming? Why don't you explain our situation to them?"

Nick could see the tears filling her eyes and as he feared, he felt immobilized by the magnitude of her emotions.

"It's just not that simple, Theresa," Nick tried to explain. "It's the law. We all have to go sooner or later. Everyone's going: me, Karl, Wolfgang, all the guys. Do you remember what *Fater* said tonight? It's my *duty* to prepare our country for war."

"Your father also said that it's important you go down and get your Master's Card. You've earned it, Nick. You've accumulated all the hours you need. And, there's the baby coming. I don't want you to go, Nick," Theresa turned her head but didn't move away from him.

Nick turned her shoulders toward him. He lifted her chin so their eyes met – *God how he loved her.* The thought of being away from her was just about killing him, but somehow,   he had to convince her that everything would be alright and they would make it through this.

"There must be a way out of this, Nick, someone to help us, maybe a form to sign or an appeal to file."

"Theresa, there is no one out there to help us. Everyone must go sooner or later, it is simply my time!" Nick felt his heart beating in his throat and knew he had better calm down before he lost his temper. Theresa was making this harder than it already was. He slammed his palm against the dresser, causing it to rattle against the wall. "You know I must go. I must! I'll get my Master's Card when I come home."

"Oh, why now?" Theresa grumbled while moving across the room, "I know you have to go, but I hate it Nick, hate it, hate it! And what happened with Katarina last year, I..." Theresa shrugged her shoulders, turning from him, trying to hide her shame.

"How many times do I have to tell you?" Nick said feeling a bit irritated at an old issue resurrected. "Katarina's death was not your fault. She was born deformed. You could not feed her."

"I know, I know, I know," Theresa moved across the room and began staring trancelike at the setting sun.

"I miss what could have been with her, Nick. I feel as if I failed her as a mother."

"Stop this, Theresa." Nick demanded and closed the distance between them. "You are punishing us for something we could not help. Doc Schultz said so himself. There was nothing we could do. We tried every way possible to feed her." Nick began to feel calm again and reached out and pulled Theresa into his arms despite her reluctance.

"Why are you dredging all this up now?" Nick slowly ran his fingers through Theresa's hair. "I don't want you getting upset and losing sleep over this, Theresa. It's not worth that."

"I can't bear it if you leave me, Nick. I'm afraid the same thing may happen to the new baby. I can't face this alone!" Theresa buried her face in her hands then laced her scalp with her fingers.

Nick took a step back, releasing his embrace, and realized what had happened. He and Theresa had become much more than husband and wife. They had become best friends. The person she trusted and relied upon the most was leaving her. There was nothing, nothing he could do or say that would change anything. He nudged her onto the window seat and nestled in next to her, pulling her close to him.

"Theresa," Nick knew at that moment what he had to say and how to say it. "I'm always going to be a part of you, no matter where I go, no matter what happens. We are connected, together, forever, remember? When I'm gone and you feel afraid, I want you to close your eyes and think of me. That's our love, Theresa. Yes, it's going to be tested, it's going to be hard. But we *can* do this, you and me."

Looking up at him, she gave him a tentative smile and brushed her lips against his. With fingers entwined, the two watched the last rays of sunlight slowly fade away.

Chapter Nine

Nick shifted in his seat, readjusting his position. The constant jostling of the train ride to Karlovatz was beginning to really irritate him. *Why did these seats have to be so uncomfortable?* He pressed the side of his head against the tiny window where a faint breeze made its way across his face. Stretching his legs out catlike in front him, he leaned back into his seat, placed one foot on top of the other, and closed his eyes. He felt lucky to have a window seat because it gave him the opportunity to watch the changing landscape, allowing his mind to wander. He thought about what lay ahead for him at Karlovatz, his future with Theresa, and about the past he left behind.

"Hey, Nick, what's going on in that head of yours? You haven't said a word since we left Calma," his buddy Karl asked, wearing a grin.

Nick was grateful that Karl had been conscripted into the army with him. They would face the next six months together, and that eased Nick's apprehension. Nick and Karl had been close friends since primary school. After their training at Karlovatz, the bond between them would strengthen even more.

Nick turned away from the window to face his friend, meeting his gaze.

"What am I thinking about?" Nick repeated Karl's question. "My *Datee*."

"Tell me about him, would you, Nick? I'm awfully bored, and we're stuck on this heap of metal all day."

Karl listened as Nick poured out the details of his father's life, things that Karl had never heard before. Nick told him that his father had lived with his aunt and uncle after both of his parents had died when he was six years old. But his father ran away when he was 12 years old, after his aunt had died.

"Where did your *Fater* go?" Karl took a large bite of a slice of sweetened bread that the porter had served moments earlier.

"He went to work at the Cutala farm, just doing menial tasks, until he moved to the Brundelick farm as master herdsman."

"He herded the cows through town?"

Nick nodded his head, agreeing with Karl. Placing their elbows on their knees, the two men leaned in toward one another.

"How long did he stay at the Brundelick place?"

"A few years after he married my mother, Eva Hoffmann. They were married at Holy Wendelin Catholic Church in 1902. He was 23 years old then."

Karl sat back in his seat and stared out their cabin window, "Nick, didn't you have a sister that died?"

Nick let his head drop a bit and stared at the floor boards beneath his feet. His right foot began playing with a nail that had worked its way up.

"Yeah, my sister Mary died of some kind of stomach problem. She was nineteen. And my brother

34

Anton died in 1909, two years before I was born. He was only six years old."

"What from?"

"I don't know," Nick said shrugging his shoulders, "Mama always said of a broken heart, because *Datee* was in the States."

"That's right; I remember your *fater* went to the States. He didn't like farming, huh?"

"No." Nick was glad to be off the topic of his brother and sister. He hadn't known Anton, but his memories of Mary were those of a kind sister who made him laugh. It still hurt to think of her.

"*Fater* didn't make enough money farming and he wanted to build us a new house, so he left for America and found work in the steel mills in Pennsylvania."

Karl shifted his weight from side to side. "How long did he stay there, Nick?"

"Uh... about a year, I guess. Then he came home started the new house around 1906. But he ran out of money. A year later he went back. This time, he stayed for three years and brought enough money back to finish the house. You knew my *Fater* fought in the war, right?"

"In 1914, after the Archduke of Austria was assassinated by the Serbs?"

"Yeah, that's right." Nick felt proud to be talking about his father and his years in the war.

"He operated an automatic machine gun. He became known as their number one gunner."

"Impressive. Too bad Austria lost that war. My *Fater* was so mad about that! Our borders changed and everything else with it. Serbs! Did your *Fater* go back to the States after that?"

"Not until 1919. Then he stayed over there for five more years. That was the last time he went over."

Karl sat back against his seat and exhaling and said, "Nick, what a story. That's something, your *Fater* going to America to find work, staying over there for years, going back over and over again! I couldn't do it, Nick. Could you?"

Nick stood up to stretch his legs. He placed both hands on the slim window frame, and stared at the changing landscape, "Me? No, I couldn't leave Theresa for that long." He then turned to face Karl. "The next six months will be hard enough for me."

"We'll be okay here, Nick. This is nothing. It's just training camp. Let's try to enjoy this."

Nick smiled and tried to punch Karl in the shoulder, but he moved too quickly dodging the blow. The two men stood facing each other, shook their heads with a grin, and returned to their seats with a thump, laughing, biding their time, feeling their anxiety drain away.

"You boys want some lunch?" a stout conductor poked his head inside the cabin.

"Hell, *ja!*" they both said in unison.

Chapter Ten

Theresa took in her surroundings. Standing outside at the train depot, she turned toward her mother-in-law.

"What time did you say the train is to arrive?" Theresa asked her mother-in-law for yet one more time. The whole family decided to go to the train station to welcome Nick home. They left nine-month-old Magdalena sleeping soundly in a crib at the neighbor's house.

"You know what time the train gets in, Theresa, 11:00, now don't ask us again."

"She's excited," Uncle Phillip said, "and who could blame her? She hasn't seen him in how long?"

"Yes, let her be," Helen joined in the lively discussion cradling Theresa in a warm embrace. "You know how close she and Nick are. They are like one person."

"Just like us, Helen." Josef winked at his wife. Helen returned the smile and joined hands with her husband.

Theresa couldn't seem to calm herself and wait patiently like the others. She found her eyes glued to the train tracks, as if the train would suddenly appear and she would miss everything. Month after month had passed since Nick had left for Karlovatz and although she received his letters, there were simply not enough of them to satisfy her. His chair at the dining room table was empty. His place in their bed lay vacant. In the beginning, she sobbed herself to sleep. Soon, she remembered Nick's advice and in her moments of greatest fear, she thought of him and the anxiety passed. She had made it. Her beautiful daughter arrived safely on May 27, 1932.

"I think I hear something," one of the onlookers shouted out.

Theresa swung her head in the direction of the excitement that suddenly took hold of the crowd. She found herself moving with them, separated from her family. People were pushing, shoving, trying to get closer to the tracks, closer to their loved ones who would be disembarking soon. The impatient crowd moaned as metal on metal protested against the conductor's command, bringing the carrier to a slow, grinding halt. Theresa covered her ears with her gloved hands and found herself lost in the crowd.

Nick looked out of every cabin window as he made his way down the narrow and crowded aisle toward the train door exit. He wanted to find Theresa but the sea of people in the train station made that impossible. He wondered how he'd find anyone. He pressed his duffel bag tightly against his chest and quickly took his allotted place in line to get off the train and back on home soil.

"Well, Nick, we made it," Karl said looking back at Nick with a broad smile.

Nick winked in agreement but secretly was glad to be done with his duty. The time at the camp did pass quickly, just as Karl had suggested. After the initial training period, Nick received his orders. Should his country ever encounter war, his assignment would be to build barracks. He would not be part of the ground combat teams. He would not become a *number one gunner* as his father had, and to be honest, Nick didn't mind one bit. He had no desire to fire a weapon; although he could if he had to. They made sure of that. He could still feel the cold metal against his skin and felt clammy thinking about it. He hoped he wouldn't *always* feel it there, on the side of his hip, as firm as a stake in the ground.

"Nick! Nick! Over here!" yelled his brother-in-law Josef, the first voice Nick heard as he stepped off the train and onto the soft dirt of Calma. He looked at the speckles of dirt that landed on his shoe and for a moment felt an ache inside. *I'm home.* He looked up to find Josef standing in front of him with a smile nothing less than genuine.

"Josef, you're a sight for sore eyes." The two men locked in a firm handshake. Nick wasn't sure how it happened, but he finally felt all grown up. He felt like a man who was ready to defend his country if he had to, and now he had the training behind him.

Before Nick could see her coming, Theresa landed in his arms, breaking the two men's embrace.

"Nick, Nick, my darling, my darling!" she uttered as she relaxed in his arms.

Nick dropped his duffel onto the ground and looked into the eyes of his wife. His heart was racing. He gently placed both hands on the side of her face and kissed her, harder than he ever had before. He could hear nothing else but her gentle moaning; the noise of the crowd, the family making small talk, it all simply faded away.

"What does a mother have to do to get a welcome from her son?"

"Mama," Nick turned, and embraced her.

Chapter Eleven

The days passed quickly as Nick settled into the old routines of home. He was sleeping better than he had in almost a year. Now he was ready to share with Theresa a decision he had made.

"I'm going to town to get my Master's Card." Nick said as he slid back into his chair. He pushed his shoulders back and felt them hit the back of the chair.

"I'm going to make the arrangements to take the examination and build my project."

Although he had earned all of his hours before leaving for military training camp, Nick still felt a little nervous about taking the examination. For as long as he could remember, he dreamed of becoming a cabinet maker and now it was just an examination away from his reach.

"Oh! Nick, that's wonderful news." Theresa smiled broadly as she wiped her hands on her apron. "Yes, yes, you should."

Nick picked up his Ledger and tucked it under his arm. He kissed Theresa good-bye and headed out across town to the tradesmen building. Nick couldn't keep the smile off of his face as he entered the building. He was excited to get the examination process started and felt more than ready for the challenge. But the feeling of elation didn't last long when he looked around the office area. Some changes had been made in his absence. Huge directional signs barked commands. The worst part about it was that they were written in Serbian, a language Nick had limited exposure to and deep down, despised. After a miserable encounter at the check-in window, Nick was directed to Mr. Stepan, the supervisor, who spoke both Serbian and German.

"I have completed the number of hours needed and recorded them in my Journeymen's Ledger here," Nick explained while raising his Ledger into plain view. "I want to sign up to take the examination for my Master's Card."

"I'm sorry young man, but we do not accept the Journeymen's Ledger anymore. There's a new system in place." Mr. Stepan was a slender, middle-aged man who appeared to be losing the battle between himself and his paper-filled desk. He leaned over to a pile of thick books on the floor, picked one up, and handed it to Nick. "First, you have to study this text. When you are finished, come back and take your examination."

"Now I have to read a book first before taking the examination?" Nick stammered. "What do you mean? I have all of my hours logged right here in this Ledger. It took years to accumulate this number of hours." Nick pounded his fist on the desk, demanding an answer.

"Keep your Ledger for yourself," Mr. Stepan instructed, waving his hands back and forth between himself and Nick. A sign of irritation emerged in a slight wrinkle that made its way across his forehead. "Where have you been that you do not know this by now?" Mr. Stepan asked while inching his thick glasses up over the bridge of his nose.

"Where have I been?" Nick repeated, swallowing hard in an attempt to control his temper. "In the army serving my country, you fool!" Nick thrust both hands toward Mr. Stepan and felt he was losing control. His Journeymen's Ledger fell to the floor next to his right foot and he kicked it hard. As the ledger flew across the room, Nick noticed that Mr. Stepan did not appear annoyed or frazzled at his outburst and assumed he had dealt with this kind of response before. He looked down to the text he was given. He opened it and began paging through it, flipping one page over, then the next. Each turn of the page went faster and faster between his fingers. His heart began racing. His anger had grown into in a full rage by now.

"This book is written in Serbian! I can't do this! I don't know the language! You must be crazy!"

"Well, you must do it because that is the way things are done now. The exam will take you all morning. Once you have completed the examination, you will be required to build a cabinet from start to finish. It must not take you more than four days. Then, maybe, you will get your Master's Card."

"But this is not fair," Nick's voice trailed off. He received no mercy from Mr. Stepan, who stood up from his desk and began ushering Nick to the exit with firmness.

"Go on now - this is the way it is son - take it or leave it!" Mr. Stepan picked up Nick's Journeymen's Ledger and handed it to Nick. He then turned on the balls of his feet, and walked back over to his desk.

Nick slammed the voluminous text shut and

shoved it under his arm, stomped down the stairs, and left the building allowing the door to close with a loud bang. *How am I going to explain this to Theresa? She told me to get my Master's Card before I left for the training camp. Why, didn't I take her advice!*

Chapter Twelve

After explaining his ordeal at the tradesmen building, Nick looked into the eyes of his father. His father had urged him to get his Master's Card before departing for Karlovatz, and Nick now felt ashamed for not taking the advice.

"Well, that's the whole story," Nick said that evening after the supper dishes had been cleared away. Nick's father was seated at the head of the table looking with intensity at Nick, devouring his every word.

"I have this damn textbook to study before being able to take the examination, and I don't know how I'm going to do it – written in Serbian, of all languages!" Nick spat out the words while spinning the textbook end to end across the table.

"I know how you are going to do it," his father replied in a commanding voice, "with my help." Nick's father pounded his finger onto the wooden table in firm, rhythmic beats. "You and I will spend our nights at this kitchen table until we make our way through it, for as long as it takes."

Nick looked up at his father. He felt defeated but at the same time knew his father would stand by his word. Nick nodded in silent agreement, picked up the book, and said goodnight.

The next two years were spent exactly as predicted. In the soft light of the lantern, the two men sat at the kitchen table, and dissected the information, making sense of the curriculum. Nick's days were spent practicing his trade working as a cabinet maker under Uncle Phillip's license. First, he helped his brother-in-law, Josef, build a masonry shop on his property. Once the shop was completed, Josef began referring his customers to Nick for cabinetry. If there was a lull, Nick picked up work helping Uncle Phillip at his shop. But that didn't happen often. Most mornings Nick rose at 3:00 a.m. and worked long after sunset just to keep up with the demand. In 1936, he decided to buy a motorcycle so he could travel between job sites quicker and with more ease.

Soon, Nick became known in the village as a fine craftsman specializing in bedroom suites, desks, cabinets, doors, windows, picture frames and caskets. Theresa added her touch to his finished pieces by painting delicate flowers and designs, giving Nick's work a signature look. As the years passed, and his reputation grew, so did their family. Nick and Theresa welcomed two more children into their home: a son, Nick, in 1934, and a daughter, Kati in 1935. Their home was filled with laughter, good food, and a paycheck from a hard day's work. When the day came for Nick to take his examination, he stood a proud man. He felt like he accomplished the impossible and was on top of the world. On July 24, 1935, he received his Master's Card and was now licensed, his dream fulfilled.

As the years passed, political unrest was brewing in Europe. Nick's concern for his young family intensified. When Germany invaded Poland in 1939, Great Britain and France declared a state of war and Nick's homeland became a target between the Allied forces and the Axis power. The Partisans, a guerilla group led by a Croatian named Josip Broz Tito, began to terrorize villages such as Calma in an attempt to thwart Germany's advances. The German army, also desiring the area, fought against the Partisans for the same reason: expansion. The people of Yugoslavia found themselves caught in the middle of a war they wanted no part of.

"*Fater*, I'm worried about what could happen here with the Partisans invading our village and the possibility of going to war with Germany," Nick shared one night after everyone else had gone to bed. The light from the lantern cast unfamiliar shadows across the kitchen walls, giving the room an eerie feel foreshadowing the events that might lie ahead.

"I know, son, but remember we have the bunker that surrounds our village and the school house armed with a few German soldiers. If the Partisans strike, that's our safe haven. Our defense plan is in place; we continue rotating shifts, standing guard over our homeland. We can't depend on anyone but ourselves. We cannot let our guard down or we're dead. It's that simple, Nick. And if Germany decides to invade us, we lose our independence as a country." Nick's father shook his head back and forth with a grimace. "We're finished. I don't know how we would come out the victor in that situation, despite the fact that we are of German heritage. We will be aligned with Germany, not Yugoslavia, from that point forward."

Nick nodded in agreement and wasn't sure which

scenario his father described would be the worse outcome. Nearby villages were suffering awful circumstances at the hands of the Partisans who came down into the villages at night from the mountain areas on killing sprees. Typically, they chose villages that appeared vulnerable and ill-equipped against their weapons of fire and guns. Germany was making huge advances across Europe and the residents of Calma knew it was only a matter of time before they would be next. Once the German armies overran an area, soldiers took up housing in villager's homes, sleeping in their beds, eating their food. Living in fear of being attacked by the Partisans or invaded by the German army was a constant weight on Nick's mind. If the German troops continued on the path they were on, Nick knew he would be drafted into the Yugoslav army. How could he protect his family if he were to be called to protect his country?

Chapter Thirteen

Nick was busy putting the finishing touches on the small armoire he had just finished when Theresa came running into Uncle Phillip's shop holding an envelope.

"You've been called back in. I know it. I know it, I know it!" she shrieked.

"Theresa calm down. You'll upset the customers." Nick nodded to an older couple chatting quietly with Uncle Phillip across the room.

"Open it," Theresa whispered as she lowered herself onto a bench nearby.

Nick toyed with the brown paper envelope that had his name inscribed on the front, moving it across his fingers. He opened the contents and read what he suspected. He had been formally conscripted into the Yugoslav army in the year 1941.

Nick looked up and met his wife's gaze and smiled. "Come here darling."

Theresa walked into his arms and held him for the longest time.

"When?"

"Ten days."

Nick boarded the train early the morning of his

departure. Unlike the ride to the military training camp, he was ushered into a box car headed for the Serbian woods. His orders were clear: identify German parachutists and report their location back to his commanding officer immediately. Nick was uncertain how the assignments were handed out, and frankly, he really didn't care. He was part of the Yugoslav Army, on the brink of war, and it felt very real.

"We're headed for Belgrade?" a young man asked. Although Nick was only 34 years old, he felt like an old man sitting next to this young soldier, who couldn't have been more than 16.

"*Ja*, Belgrade, but we have to change trains soon. Just follow me."

The cattle car shuddered along the track as it traveled north over the Sava River. Through the cracks, cold spring air swirled throughout the car. Nick shuddered and admitted to himself that he wasn't as comfortable as he pretended to be to the young soldier. He wondered what to expect in the months ahead, what type of man his commanding officer would be, and if he would be able to do his job well. Sitting on the wooden planked floor among his unit, he wished to be anywhere but where he was. He dropped his head onto his knees in a huddle position trying to keep warm, forced his eyes closed, and listened to the cadenced beating of train and track.

Hours passed in excruciating slowness. Finally, the train reached its destination. Nervous chatter broke out among the men. They smoothed their hair as if to make an impression and grabbed their duffels. Attempting light conversation seemed silly to Nick. It wasn't going to get any better. He stood up and stretched out his back. The young man who he had been talking to earlier was right on his heels. Someone outside began banging on the door, prying it open with what sounded like a heavy metal rod. The reverberation was ear drum piercing. The door cracked open and sunlight streamed into the car along with the icy spring air of a late April afternoon. Men started slapping at their thighs to quicken the dust and dirt off of them. Somewhere in the distance, an animal howled, sending chills up Nick's spine. He was uncertain why, but his discomfort was growing. Apprehension merged with anxiety, causing his adrenaline to surge. He could feel that heavy knot forming in his stomach whenever he became anxious. Nick grabbed his belongings and stared straight ahead as if preparing for bad news. The door slammed up against the door jamb and stopped abruptly in a thunderous, banging halt. The men groaned, moving away from the unwanted clatter of wood and metal.

Since he was one of the last to board the train, Nick now found himself at the front of the pack. He didn't cower back; instead, he stood his ground. He squinted against the setting sun that was now pouring into the train car. He took a few steps forward, landing on the wooden gangplank structure. With his feet now planted firmly on solid ground, he looked around and took in his new surroundings. Trying to regain his focus from the dank environment, he found himself looking square into the eyes of a Serbian soldier. At once, the soldier took a bold step forward, pointed his finger at Nick, and shouted without hesitation, "Shoot him. He's with Hitler."

Nick could feel his pulse pounding in his throat. He dropped his bag onto the dock, causing a small patch of dust to rise at his feet. In his peripheral vision, he could see his fellow countrymen taking a step back in fear of the worst. Raising both hands in the universal noncombat signal, he slowly turned to reveal the insignia on his uniform. The officer took a step back, hit the shoulder of his comrade, and broke out in hearty laughter.

Nick flinched, but showed no other reaction to the officers' response. He said nothing to them and forced himself to feel nothing. If he let himself take in the degradation, he couldn't trust how he would react, and feared he might do something to place his fellow countrymen in harm's way. Sensing that the immediate danger had passed, he picked up his duffel, turned away from the officers' cackling, and said, "Come on kid, we have a job to do."

Despite the efforts of the Yugoslav Army to protect itself against German invasion, the mighty war machine invaded on Easter Sunday, April 6, 1941. Eleven days later, Yugoslavia surrendered. Nick soon found himself back home in anticipation of the next time he would have to leave his family and fight for his country. The only difference was that now he would be a member of the German Army, supporting their efforts, and their cause. Nick was made to understand that his refusal to join the new regime would mean he was a Communist, which meant his death. He had seen the truth of that warning for himself in the brutal slayings and hangings of many of the Partisans. They now lay dead, hands over hands, feet over feet in wagons to be hauled off and buried in mass graves. The once quiet village that Nick knew as a child was now infiltrated with German officers. New laws were enforced. One in particular affected Nick's family directly: all village residents were mandated to have a guest room available for German soldiers. Two of those soldiers were now living in Nick's home, sleeping in *his* bed, eating *his* food, using *his* family's things. The thought of it made Nick sick as he spat into the dirt.

Although some comfort came to the residents with the presence of the army, the threat of being attacked by the Partisans was still very much a part of their lives. The Communist guerilla group would attack at night, coming down from the mountains with guns and homemade grenades. With Nick's days numbered until his next departure, his anxiety grew for his family who would be left behind in a war-torn country.

"What have you heard, Nick?" his father asked one night.

""I'm told we will be divided by trade," Nick shared with his father. "Because I'm a cabinet maker, I'll go with the engineers."

"There will be resentment from some of the other soldiers. You need to prepare yourself, son."

Nick nodded. "*Ja*, most of the Serbs will be on the front lines."

"Where are they sending you?"

"To the woods, to build barracks and repair bridges."

"Don't cause any trouble – keep your nose clean, do you hear me?"

"Yes sir." Nick agreed, looking directly into the

eyes of his father. He had learned his lesson ignoring his father's advice once when he didn't get his Master's Card before departing for Karlovatz. It took him two long years of studying a new language before he was able to take the examination and receive his license. He didn't plan on making another mistake this time.

For the next few years, Nick rebuilt bridges, constructed new barracks, and took his father's advice. He was quiet as he went about his work, a bit of a loner, but kept his ears open and his eyes curious. Germany's advances in the Soviet Union in the west, conquering France, and battling Great Britain in the east, were staggering. The fighting seemed to be everywhere. As Germany continued its sweep across Europe, the Partisans' night raids became more violent. With most of the men at war, the village was under the protection of the very old men and the too-young-to-know-how-to fight. A few German soldiers created a safe haven at the local schoolhouse, but reaching it in the midst of an attack would be difficult. The Partisans targeted the men, but occasionally women and children were injured or killed as well. As ruthless and savage as the Partisans were, the villagers remained terrified. Once the men were eliminated, the school house became more vulnerable. If they could overtake the Germans, the village would be in their control.

Chapter Fourteen

It was 1944, and almost a year since Nick had been home on his last leave. He couldn't wait to see his family again. As he entered Calma, he noticed the village looked the same but there was an undercurrent he couldn't quite put his finger on. He knew there were German soldiers in the village setting up headquarters in the schoolhouse. He pushed the thought from his mind and looked up into the sky. Walking quickly, he passed all the familiar places he visited as a child and he headed straight for home. All he wanted was to feel the arms of his wife around him, to see the faces of his children, and hear the voices of his parents.

"Mama?" Nick asked as he stepped into the house.

"Nick!" Nick's mother made her way across the room in a few quick steps wrapping her arms around her son. *God it felt good.* Theresa descended the stairs, took one look at Nick and opened her arms to welcome her husband home. It was a wonderful reunion and the family celebrated over dinner, enjoying each other's lively conversation.

That evening the family gathered in the living room. A pelting rain was slamming against the house and the children seemed to jump with each rumble of thunder.

"So, who wants to hear a little music?" Nick's asked looking into the eyes of his children.

"We do. We do," Leni, Nick, and Kati yelped, with their smiling, young faces looking up at their father. Nick turned and picked up his button-box accordion that was leaning against the wall in its familiar spot. He had been playing the instrument since he was a young man, simply learning it on his own. It wasn't unusual for him to make merriment for the family in the evening. It helped to soothe the children and brought smiles to the faces of the adults, and sometimes, even a little dance. Theresa and Nick's mother were busy talking softly in the kitchen while preparing a light snack and some tea. Suddenly, out of nowhere, Theresa screamed, "Nick, Nick!" Without realizing it, Theresa loosened her grip on the tea kettle. It dropped to the floor, spilling hot, steamy water that spread in every direction.

Nick jumped up and set the accordion back in its place against the wall and darted into the kitchen. "What is it, Theresa? What?" Nick felt on edge. The displaced feeling he had felt earlier that day hadn't left him yet and it was beginning to gnaw away at his nerves. Theresa stood dumfounded. Nick followed her gaze out the kitchen window. A sea of gunfire lit up the sky.

"Partisans!" he shouted.

He back pedaled in the direction of the kitchen lantern and doused the light.

"Father, make out the lights," Nick stammered.

At once, the house was dark. Soft murmurs from the children were quickly silenced by the deep, soft tones of Nick's father's voice.

Nick grasped the hands of his mother and Theresa and spoke cautiously, "Theresa, Mama, listen to me. We need to get to the schoolhouse. If we can't make it, we'll run through the vineyard to the field and hide under the cornstalks. Now the rain has stopped outside, so we'll use the moonlight and fence line to guide us."

Theresa nodded and squeezed Nick's hand in affirmation, but Nick noticed his mother didn't reply.

"Mama?" Nick searched for the eyes of his mother.

Although it was dark in the house, the moonlight fell into the room through the kitchen window. Nick could see the outline of his Mama's face, the softened lines that only time could embellish. He suddenly realized how frail she truly was and felt a real sense of fear. She remained quiet but Nick could feel in her fingertips how painful this was for her. She squeezed his hand and then let it go, her arms dropping to her sides. Nick could hear the shuffling of his father's feet and accompanying cane hit the floor as he made his way over to him.

"We're not going, son."

"What do you mean, you're not going?" Nick turned to face his father, now thankful for the darkness.

"Mother and I are staying right here at home. We are not fit to run. We've had our time. But you and Theresa … you both are young and you have a family to protect, your future."

"*Fater*! No…" Nick tried to walk over to the coat rack to get his father's coat.

"Go, Nick!" His father interrupted in a commanding voice. "Go now before it's too late. We'll take care of things here."

Nick could feel the tears streaming down his face but knew he was out of time. He ran both of his hands through his hair, lacing his fingers behind his neck. Theresa stood waiting for his lead.

"Go son, save yourselves."

Nick looked into the eyes of the father he had admired all of his life and knew once again to heed his advice. The two men embraced in a fierce hug and swore to each other this was not the end. As frightening as it was, the young family put on their coats and headed out, leaving their dear ones behind.

"We'll be here when you get back." Nick heard his father shout, as the door closed behind him.

Chapter Fifteen

The night was cold and the earlier rain left a damp feel to the darkness that awaited them. The wind whipped up and curled around Nick's neck, slapping against his face. He grimaced and pressed on.

"Look at the fence line, Theresa. Do you see it – over there?" Nick pointed to the wobbly outline where the line of trees stood. The family began running together into the dark abyss, making their way to the school house across the village.

At once, it felt as if they were running straight into the gunfire. Shots seemed to be coming from everywhere, yet no one was visible. Fires split the pitch blackness like a sheet flapping in the wind. Nick soon realized they must have been setting the hay bales on fire. Soon, tepees of smoke rose from the ground, snapping and hissing as they burned. The gunfire became louder as the Partisans overran the village. The family had been running for nearly 30 minutes now, the children often stumbling but quickly aided by one of their parents. Nick knew they were headed for trouble.

"We're not going to make it!" Nick yelled to his family. "Get into the house." Nick pointed at a nearby dark house hoping to find safety for his family.

Opening the door, they stepped into house, raced

down a narrow hallway and entered the living room. Nick immediately began hiding his precious family. Theresa and Leni were placed behind a large couch. Nicky and Kati were behind the wood carrier. He was about to join them when he thought he spotted movement across one of the back windows. It wasn't until it happened a second time that his suspicion was confirmed.

"Ssshh,"Nick instructed as he stretched out both of his arms. "Everyone, quiet," he insisted. Theresa and the children immediately stopped moving and looked at him for direction. Crouching down he slowly lowered himself effortlessly to the floor. They waited. Holding their breath, praying they had not been seen, hoping to be forgotten.

The door swung open and banged against the wall, causing the windows to shudder. Leni gasped but was silenced with pressure from her mother's hand. Heavy feet entered the hallway. Floorboards creaked from the sudden weight. The footsteps got louder and louder. Then, another set of feet entered the house and another, and another. Panic stricken, Nick realized they had been found out. The Partisans were headed right for them.

"I know some of them are in here," a gruff voice said. "I saw them come in. Find them, now!"

Nick knew there was only one chance of escape before the soldiers entered the room.

"Everyone, run," he shouted and pointed to a back door just a few feet away. Running, tripping, and dragging each other through the doorway and down the steps, they made their way out of the building, and back into the dark night.

"Run toward the vineyard," Nick shouted, "the vineyard!"

Nick turned toward the soldiers who were closing the distance between them. He forced his eyes to focus on what he feared was happening. It appeared to him that the soldier closest to them was setting a homemade grenade. Nick could see his family ahead of him by several yards, but he still felt the imminent danger that the grenade now presented. Homemade grenades were unpredictable, lethal, and often times, deadly. Nick's training had prepared him for this moment. He wasn't afraid; instead, he felt a controlled rage as he continued running and yelled until out of breath, "No!"

Chapter Sixteen

It felt like a thousand little needles, the sharp, burning sensation that grazed Nick's shoulder. His legs felt as if they were flailing far ahead of the rest of his body. As his feet dug into the wet dirt, he thrust himself forward with all of his might. His eyes burned as he fought his way through the smoky haze. He could hear the soldiers behind him but sensed they were no longer close. The grenade had exploded into a small hill, spewing grass, dirt, and tiny bits of metal in every direction. The smoke and fine soot that followed created a timely veil for escape.

Nick caught up to his family within moments, "Get under the cornstalks and stay there."

One by one the family fell to their knees and crawled under the protection of the bound stalks.

"Are you hurt? Have you been hit?" Theresa asked in labored breaths.

Nick's heart was drumming in his ears. He couldn't catch his breath. He grabbed a handful of the dirt, thankful to be alive, and squeezed it between his fingers.

"Is *Datee* hurt? *Datee, Datee?"* the children couldn't help from screaming.

"I'm okay, darlings. I'm okay." He ripped part of

his sleeve to use as a makeshift bandage then closed his eyes against the stabbing pain. "Be silent," he said.

The family spent the night and awoke the next day to the sound of gunfire again. Nick peered through the stalks to see the neighboring village men pitching in to help fight the battle. When it was finally clear and safe to emerge, Nick felt angry and degraded.

"How is that wound?" Theresa asked.

Nick knew he wouldn't be able to hide it any longer.

"It's okay, Theresa; maybe Doc Schultz can take a look at it, but this has got to end. We can't go on living like this."

"I know, Nick, but this is our home, our children's home." Theresa thrust both of her fists into her apron pockets but Nick could feel her eyes surveying his shoulder.

"Not anymore." He looked at Theresa knowing that he had reached his limit. He had to make a plan for his family and intended to discuss it with his father as soon as the time was right. Theresa became quiet, following Nick's lead step-for-step, back to the house.

Nick was overwhelmed with relief to find his parents unharmed. The family insisted that Dr. Schultz stop by to examine Nick's wound. As soon as the visit was over, Nick decided he would broach the subject of leaving Calma with his father.

"The pieces are in too deep, Nick; they're going to have to stay there." Dr. Schultz stood up and began packing up his instruments back into his black medical bag. The bag creaked shut. He pushed the lever over with his thumb, securing the contents.

"What do you mean, stay there?" Nick asked, clearly irritated.

"Eventually, they'll work their way out, but it could take years."

Nick moaned, swaying his head from side to side. The last thing he wanted to carry inside of him was Partisan grenade shrapnel. He thanked Doc Schultz for his service, attempted to shake his hand, but immediately winced instead. The two men parted and Nick headed outside to find his father. He wanted a plan in place for his family before he was called back to active duty.

"*Fater*, there is talk about an evacuation if Belgrade falls to the Partisans. I think we had better get ready to leave Calma. If Germany plans a retreat, it won't take long and the Partisans will overrun the village. Their numbers are growing – we've seen that from the attack the other night. Damn communists," Nick said under his breath.

"Be careful with that kind of talk, Nick," he placed both of his hands lightly on Nick's shoulders as if to stop him from moving forward, "it could get you killed."

Nick nodded, but his emotions for the Partisans remained firm. He was afraid to admit it but he had a real sense of fear for his family.

"As much as I hate to think about it," Nick's father stood and rubbed the back of his neck, "I agree with you. If you've heard that an evacuation is being planned that means we're getting close to real danger. The town crier has been good about keeping us informed on what's going on out there. If the Germans pull out of the school house, we're in real trouble. We've lost our defense. It's going to be very hard for us to leave everything behind and start all over again. All those trips I made to America to earn money to finish our house – it will all be lost once we leave Calma."

Nick could sense that his father had strong feelings about leaving Calma, and he understood those feelings completely. This was going to be the single most difficult task his family would have to do. It would mean packing up whatever they could fit into his parents' covered wagon and leaving Calma, probably forever. *Why did it have to come to this? We're being driven right out of our homes and walking into ... what?*

"Nick, have you heard about the government relocation program?" Nick's father asked, bringing Nick out of the fog he found himself in.

"*Ja*. You mean the relocation program in Wernstein? Maybe that's how we should look at this from now on, a fresh start in our Austria, our family's homeland." Nick replied.

"*Ja*, your grandfather was born in Austria-Hungary."

Nick and his father found themselves discussing the details of their escape quite frequently over the next week. The more they talked about it, the more it felt to Nick that his family would be leaving Calma.

"Now," his father started in one night, "Your mother and I will pack up the wagon and go to Wernstein. Theresa and the children will take the truck to the train station in the next village. From there, they travel to Dresden until we send for them. Their train tickets include room and board in government housing."

"*Ja*, okay," Nick took in the details he knew he

would have to remember in order to find his family in the future.

"As soon as we can," Nick's father continued, "we'll send Uncle Phillip for them. He's planning on joining us. He'll get to Wernstein before we will and he'll have the opportunity to settle in. Right now, I think we've got to butcher the pigs and start thinking about what to take and what we must leave behind."

"*Fater*, I'm so afraid I won't be here to help." Nick confessed to his father. "My leave is up soon."

"Nick, don't worry about us – we can handle this. You take care of yourself now. Do you hear me, son?"

"*Ja*, but it turns my stomach to think about the Partisans taking over our village. Their filthy hands will be on everything. All will be lost or destroyed by them." Nick said in disgust. He rubbed the back of his hand across his forehead not realizing he had started to perspire. Thinking about the Partisans pilfering through his private things made Nick's blood boil. He had heard enough about how other villages were literally ransacked when the Partisans overran them. The German citizens lost all of their rights, to own property or their businesses; instead, they were forced to work as slaves or shipped to Russian labor camps.

Deep down, Nick harbored a suspicion that the family would have to leave without him. It was an unsettling thought: his family on the run while he served in the war. But he was powerless to change anything. A fire began to burn within him. Was it revenge? Was it fear? Nick bit the side of his cheek realizing something was brewing in the pit of his stomach. He had to make it right for his family as soon as he had the chance.

Chapter Seventeen

Nick's suspicions proved to be true. Shortly after he returned to active duty in 1944, Belgrade was overrun by Partisan forces, and the German army driven out. The threat of invasion to the east was now great. In October, the Calma town crier made an announcement that would affect Nick and his family forever: a German military truck would evacuate all Germans who had no other way out. They would be transported to the train depot in the next village and would travel to Dresden by boxcar. If they chose to stay behind, they risked being captured by the Partisans, which likely meant torture, even death.

Early one morning, the sound of a heavy military truck entered the village followed by the hard beating of the town crier's drum. "Two hours - you have two hours – to get out!" he cried out over and over again.

Family by family, the Germans left their homes and climbed aboard the truck. The old people eased themselves down slowly onto the dirty, wooden floor. Theresa and the children were the last to board. They stood, huddled together in a small group, each one holding onto a small blanket that held a few of their belongings.

"Mommee, Mommee," the children pleaded as their eyes sought out hers for comfort.

Theresa buried her fears, "It's going to be all right, children," she repeated over and over again, making an effort to touch each one, as the truck pulled away from Calma.

As soon as Theresa and the children were safely on the truck and headed for Dresden, Nick's parents climbed onto their packed wagon and left. They suspected an evacuation was coming, so they packed up early in anticipation. The family had prepared exactly as Nick and his father had planned: they butchered their pigs, fried the meat, and preserved it layer by layer in big containers of lard. They pressed sacks of flour into nooks and crannies of the wagon, secured by their preserves, dried vegetables, their pots and pans. They packed up bedding and clothing, a few dishes, lanterns and the most precious of mementos. The rest of their possessions were left behind, lost forever.

Now it was time for them to leave, for good. They waved farewell to their Serbian and Croatian friends who stayed behind knowing they might never again set eyes on them, or their village, again as long as they lived.

Calma took on a new look as the German people departed in a mass exodus. Homes stood with no signs of life within. Businesses were abandoned. Farms were left for new hands to tend. The dreams and futures of the German people in Calma went up in smoke overnight, dismantled before their eyes, with the simple warning from the town crier, *you have two hours to get out!*

Theresa and the children endured the two-day trip to Dresden and settled in the relief camp where they stayed for two weeks waiting for Uncle Phillip to come and take them to Wernstein. Nick's parents safely arrived in Wernstein and in early November they sent Uncle Phillip for Theresa and the children. He arrived in Dresden and located the school house where they were housed. He carried with him a small backpack of supplies, including a large loaf of Austrian bread and canned meat assuming food would be hard for them to come by in the relief camps. The three children were given hefty portions first, then the adults ate. Once they were finished, Uncle Phillip helped them pack up the few belongings. They boarded a train destined for Passau, Austria, just an hour's walk away from Wernstein.

Chapter Eighteen

Word spread quickly through the barracks that Germany had lost the war. As soon as Nick had the chance, he pulled one of his closest friends aside.

"I knew when Paris was liberated it was over," Nick said feeling confident now that the war was over.

"*Ja*, then Russia driving them out of the Ukraine and Poland." Heinz added, "It was the beginning of the end for Hitler."

"What do you think about his suicide?"

"After Mussolini, what did you expect?"

"Oh, *Ja*, the Partisans had their way with him, didn't they? They gave him a real execution."

The two men nodded their heads in agreement.

"Where will you go now that the war is over, Heinz?" It was May 1945.

"My family should be in Dresden. We can't go home, Nick. Home is gone."

"*Ja*, I know. I'm headed for Wernstein."

"In Austria. You'll like it there Nick."

The two men shook hands and looked into each other's eyes, each realizing that although Germany had lost the war, they had won. They had endured and survived the ugliness of it all.

"*Auf Wiedersehen*, my friend," Nick said,

offering his hand.

"*Auf Wiedersehen*, Nick."

Nick's release processing went smoothly, he held his papers in his hand, picked up his duffel, and set out for the train station. He boarded the first train out and found a seat near the back. He slid in next to an older gentlemen hoping for peace and quiet so he could think.

"Where are you headed?" the older gentlemen asked.

"Passau then Wernstein."

The traveler looked at him as if needing more information in order to understand what Nick had said.

"My family is there now."

The stranger raised his eyebrows when hearing the word, *now*. "Relocation?"

"*Ja*, that's right." Nick noticed how the man surveyed his uniform. His eyes stopped at the pin Nick wore on his lapel, identifying him as part of the German Army.

"Where are you from, soldier?"

"Calma."

"Tito's communist party has taken over all of Yugoslavia now."

Nick winced, giving away his feelings on the subject.

"I'm sorry, soldier."

Nick nodded, accepting the stranger's sentiment.

"It's pretty nice over there in Wernstein, not too much damage."

"So I've heard," Nick replied. He wanted the conversation to end so he could sort things out. He leaned his head back against his seat and closed his eyes.

Fingers entwined on his lap, he thought about the last four years he had spent in the German Army. He thought about the war finally being over and returning home and was instantly overcome with a tremendous feeling of profound loss: loss of years that had been spent in the war, the loss of his homeland with the inability to really go home, and the loss of comrades in the brutality he had seen. Then he saw Theresa. Her smiling face, her warm hands touching him, and he fell sound asleep.

The shrill train whistle woke Nick with a start. For a moment, he felt he was right back in the war, running for cover.

"You okay there, son?" The kind gentlemen he had been talking to earlier was offering a hand.

"*Ja, Ja*" Nick mumbled, straightening his jacket, and clearing his throat. "I must have dozed off."

"Well, this is our stop. Welcome to Passau, Germany. Good luck to you, soldier." They exchanged a firm handshake and began gathering their personal items.

Chapter Nineteen

Stepping off the train, Nick looked around at his new surroundings. He drew in a deep breath and surveyed the small farming community. Nick was quick to admire how untouched Passau was compared to most cities in Germany. He had seen immense damage, especially in the larger cities that now lay in ruins and despair. Their streets, like those in Dresden, now impassible, were cluttered with enormous concrete boulders spewed like marbles among shattered glass, nails, wire and endless piles of wood. Once beautiful buildings, homes, or dance halls were now considered debris to be hauled away and disposed of. Good drinking water was scarce, food even more so.

People were desperate, starving, and feeling betrayed by the country that sold them the idea that the Third Reich was the superior power, immune to defeat. Now in the aftermath of the war, Nick learned that nearly two million civilians and four million German servicemen had been killed. Close to 12 million people were displaced. Millions were pouring into Germany and Austria. Many, like Nick's family, had fled their homelands to avoid Communist occupation. Some had left their villages that were simply uninhabitable. Others were prisoners of war or survivors of Nazi concentration or labor camps who aimlessly moved from village to village with the wandering look of the truly lost. The images haunted Nick, playing over and over in his mind.

Nick closed his eyes and shook his head back and forth to clear his mind and return to the present. The sound of friendly conversation caught his attention. He noticed a few of the locals chatting at the Catholic Church on the corner.

"Can we help you, soldier?"

"*Ja*, I am looking for the Relief Administration Center." Nick asked feeling his excitement building. A wide smile spread across his face. "Can you tell me where I may find it?"

"Of course, it's just down the road a bit. It's the big building at the end of the road"

"Are you far from home young man?"

"*Ja*, from Yugoslavia but my family is here now and I'm trying to find them."

"Oh, *Ja*, *Ja*, so many of your people are relocating, even to Brazil and Argentina. Good luck to you."

Since the village was quite small, it didn't take Nick long to locate the Center. He took the steps two-by-two and entered the building. To his surprise, the friendly gentlemen he had spoken to turned out to be one of the assistants at the center who once again offered him reassuring words, a kind smile, and directions to find his family. An hour later, Nick knew that his family had been sent, a farm located just outside the village of Wernstein. Pleased with his progress, he smiled realizing just how long it had been since he felt happy about something. He swung his bag over his shoulder and set out on foot immediately for the farmhouse. He was going home.

Chapter Twenty

It was dark by the time Nick finally reached his destination. The walk across the border into Austria took him longer than he anticipated. His feet ached and his back was tight. It had been a long day, and he was bone tired and God-awful hungry. He made his introductions to Mrs. Becham, a widow and the lady of the house, and was told to use the staircase in front of the home to reach the second floor. It was there that his family was living. Lifting one leg after the other, his boots fell hard on the wooden steps in a step-shuffle, step-shuffle rhythm.

"Theresa, Theresa! Nick is coming!"

Teresa's eyes popped open. The house had been silent for nearly an hour when all of a sudden she heard Nick's mother yelling.

"Nick?" Theresa whispered. Pushing the comforter up and off of her, she slipped out of her bed and began running to the other side of the room to greet her husband.

And there he stood, tired, dirty, wet and mud-spattered, but smiling.

"Children! Wake up! Your *datee* is home."

At once, Nick heard the clambering of his children's feet, saw the smiling faces of his parents, and felt the warm embrace of his wife. He was home in the summer of 1945.

Nick rose early the next morning. He was seated at the kitchen table nibbling off the crisp edges of his plum-filled *kipfel*. He turned his attention to watch Theresa preparing coffee and decided to surprise her with a kiss. Sneaking up behind her, he moved quickly across the room. Spinning her around to face him, he pulled her into his arms, and pressed his lips softly against hers. Immediately, he felt her hesitation and sensed something was wrong. He drew back, looked into her eyes, and saw something there that concerned him.

"Theresa, what is it?" He asked softly.

Theresa shook her head from side to side. "You don't know what we went through, Nick. It was horrible, horrible."

"Tell me, Theresa. Tell me it all."

For the next hour, Nick listened as Theresa shared the details of their exodus from Calma. He held back the myriad of questions that shot through his head as she spoke. He could sense she needed to tell him this story. She needed him to be silent, to just listen. She spoke of letting go of Calma, the dreams they had for their future, the heartbreak of saying goodbye as she stood alone with her children. She told him about the week-long journey his parents had to endure to get to Wernstein. He absorbed her worries as if his own as she explained how she prayed they would have enough food, water, and safe passage.

"And you, Theresa? How did it go for you and the children?"

She tried holding back her emotions as she talked through her tears. She shared with him that she lived every day, every moment, in fear of being killed by the Partisans.

"It started right away when we left Calma in the military trucks," she stuttered. "The Germans came early in the morning on October 15."

"On Kati's birthday?"

"Yes, on our little girl's birthday. They woke us from our beds, yelling at us over and over again, that we had only two hours to get on the trucks or we would be left behind. We climbed up into the filthy truck and stood there, hanging onto each other, until we reached the train depot. But it's when we passed through Galdopusta that frightened me the most. I couldn't stop from shaking, Nick. And the children, they cried, 'Mommy, Mommy are you all right?' I didn't want them to know how frightened I was, but I couldn't hide it."

"Why did they have to take you through Galdopusta? Didn't they know it was overrun by the Partisans? Surely, they had more sense than to place all of you in such danger."

"I don't know, Nick. I don't know. When we finally reached the village we had to wait for three days for the trains to arrive. We were given one meal a day. When the trains did come for us they were boxcars, Nick! There were no benches, no seats. We sat on the cold, wooden floor like animals! When the doors would open to let more people onto the train, we begged for food from those outside, but no one, no one gave us anything!" Theresa cried. "They looked at us as if we were gypsies."

"Oh, Theresa, I had no idea."

"So many times, the trains would come to a

screeching halt. We were ordered to get off and run for the bunkers because the American pilots were coming. It was an air raid, Nick! We ran and ran and ran for our lives and lay in the cold dirt. Before the air raid, I lost Nicky. I couldn't find him until it was all over. It was so frightening." Theresa moved across the room, sat down lightly into a chair, and slumped over, a look of exhaustion on her face having relived the horror. Nick sat for a moment speechless, slowly realizing what his family had gone through to get where they were today. He followed her path and took his seat back at the kitchen table, bracing himself for the rest of the story.

"And the relief camp was no better – we were told we would be sharing one large area and to use huge pieces of old tattered fabric to divide the families. We were so hungry, Nick. The children were so hungry. I brought home dark beer for them to drink. God, forgive me."

"What do you mean, you brought home dark beer? Where were you?"

"They came for me."

"Who? Who came for you, Theresa?" Nick felt the slightest ebb of irritation and loosened the collar of his shirt as if to relieve a building pressure.

"The German soldiers, they took me to work at an ammunition factory during the day in Dresden!"

"Ammunition factory?" Nick stood up, his chair slammed against the wall, then fell onto the floor. "The Americans were bombing the ammunition factories!! How could they do this to my family? They were supposed to protect you, not use you for labor and place you in harm's way!"

Nick calmed himself down, took a few steps over to Theresa, and knelt down to meet her gaze. He grabbed hold of both her hands and held them tight within his. He now understood the burden she had been carrying and feared it would be something she would hold inside of her forever. His only hope was that she wouldn't hold it against him.

"Theresa, thank God you are alive. Thank God." Nick knew that the city of Dresden was heavily bombed just a few months after his family left for Wernstein. The allies destroyed 39 square kilometers of the city in an attempt to annihilate the railroad and especially the ammunition factories. Later, the city was burned to the ground, a complete shambles with so many dead. He wiped new tears that began to fall down his cheeks and closed his eyes for God's grace in sparing his wife and children from a fate so many other German citizens endured. He vowed to himself to make things right again and remembered his father's words from his boyhood, "If you ever get the chance to go to America, Nick, go."

Chapter Twenty-one

Later that day, Nick found himself walking around the property he would soon call home. A small two-story house was set back from the dirt road. Nick and his family occupied the second floor of the homestead. They were given one large room where the beds lined the walls like a row of train tracks, one after the other. A small stove and table stood alone in the corner. Meals were eaten downstairs with Mrs. Becham and her daughter, but the group did not share food. Instead, each family had to provide for its own. Sunday visits to the butcher supplied soup bones, bacon, or sausage, staples that were stretched to last a week's time.

Smoke slowly curled a path out of the stout chimney. Nick noticed now what he couldn't see last night, a weakened wooden fence quarantined the home. The livestock had separate stations along the path of the fence line. Cow stalls stood underneath a rusted tin shed. He heard the cackling sounds of chickens and could smell the pungent odors wafting up from a nearby pig sty. A single horse stood crunching on oats while a few ducks meandered beneath him pecking at the grains that managed to escape from the mighty jaws. It was a peaceful, beautiful place.

Nick was beginning to feel better than he had in

days. He wanted to believe that this little farmhouse in Austria could be a good place for his family to heal and for him to finally let go of the cold heart of war. He also knew this government-mandated arrangement would not be long-term. He wanted more for his family, much more, and now as head of this family, it was up to him to provide it.

Over the next several weeks, Nick and Uncle Phillip got busy and found work as cabinet makers in the next village. It was a two-mile walk and they made sure a lunch was included in a day's pay. Food had become a constant hardship for the family, and if Nick could manage a meal away from home, it relieved the burden. Nick began to take notice of the condition of Mrs. Becham's farm: the worn wooden cabinets and doors, the weakened animal stalls, and the broken-down porch. Nick figured her standard of living had been in decline since the death of her husband. Nick played around with an idea in his head until he had the opportunity to present it to Mrs. Becham. Over the next several years, Nick would repair and replace doors, cabinets, and armoires. He renewed the porch, which included the staircase, the cow stalls, and just about everything else that was made of wood. In return, he would earn bacon, flour, egg-laying chickens, ducks, milk, cheese and on occasion, precious meat. After a short time, Nick could see the rewards of his idea on the supper table and in the faces of his children.

The family also benefited from a small piece of land in which to make a garden. Theresa went to work immediately planting potatoes, onions, carrots and other root vegetables that grew well in the Austrian soil.

Nick's mother contributed as well making frequent trips to the horse slaughterhouse for scraps for soup. When this was served alongside a thick slice of Austrian bread, sprinkled with a bit of salt and paprika, Nick thought he was in heaven. As time passed, the family began to heal, both physically and emotionally.

More and more village residents from Calma began to settle in Wernstein and life began to feel like old times. The annual dances drew villagers together and day by day, little by little, people began to smile again. But, in the fall of 1947, Nick was faced with a situation that would demand change.

"It's time for your daughter Leni to begin working on the farm." Mrs. Becham remarked one night as Nick was walking up the stairs from a long day's work. "If she works, I can get more food rations for your family."

"Leni is only 15," Nick complained.

"*Ja*, that is old enough to be working full-time on the farm. She can start milking the cows and cutting the grass.

"How can she do this? I cannot help her," Nick explained. He shrugged his shoulders and waited for Mrs. Becham's response.

"She doesn't need help. I can see she is a healthy girl with a strong back. She will learn to use the scythe. She can fill the sacks with the cut grass and throw them up onto the wagon. The cows need to eat or we'll have no milk, no butter, no cream!" she scolded.

Nick was furious. He did not want his daughter, Leni, to be working as a field hand. He prided himself on being a tradesman and providing for his family. Despite his reluctance, he knew he had to agree with Mrs. Becham. They needed the ration tickets. Nick had no choice.

"Very well then. I will speak with her tonight," Nick reluctantly replied.

"Tell her I will expect her in the morning. She should meet me in the milking barn at 4 a.m."

Nick wanted to protest, but he knew it would be useless to argue. This was the arrangement the family had agreed to when moving here, and if they didn't like it, they would have to leave.

"*Ja.*" Nick gritted, cursing between his teeth, as he headed inside.

Chapter Twenty-two

Months passed. Leni was miserable in her new role as a farm hand. Nick knew something had to change or the quality of their lives would continue to descend.

"Today, I heard about better jobs over in Salzburg." Nick said, sitting at the supper table one night.

"Salzburg?" Nick Sr. asked. He placed his fork down slowly onto the kitchen table and said, "Salzburg is known as the town of festivals. It is stunning. The steeples in the village are colored like tin. It's a wonderful city."

"Maybe we should give it a try, Nick" Theresa urged. "We will never have our own home working like this, and poor Leni, doing a man's work at 15."

"*Ja*," Nick agreed with his wife, "maybe we can get off this farm and into better jobs."

"Yes, *Datee*, go and see if you can get new jobs for us." Leni was eager to leave behind the farmhand work she was doing. She poked at the blisters that now laced her palms.

"*Ja*, okay." Nick agreed and began to give it more thought.

Nick made two trips to Salzburg over the next month. Both times, he returned home and had to look into the eyes of his family to tell them the bad news. He was unsuccessful. The sea of people trying to secure better jobs and housing was astonishing. Nearly a half a million people flooded Austria alone since the war had ended. Nick began to rethink how to reach those who could help him and came up with a solution. He decided to bribe his way in by offering a slab of bacon, a large block of butter, and a round dark loaf of Austrian bread. Maybe gifting his way in to the people in charge would result in success.

"What did you say your name was?" A pale face stared back at Nick from across a large metal desk. His nametag read *Herr* Schmidt. He pushed aside the papers that cluttered his table top, pulling the dark loaf of Austrian bread in front of him. After he wrapped his nimble fingers around the wooden handle of the bread knife, he carefully began cutting a thick slice from the loaf.

"Nicholas. Nicholas Russ."

Herr Schmidt opened his mouth wide, sinking his teeth into the fluffy delicacy, "Hmmm."

Nick was uncertain if he was commenting on the bread or reacting to his name.

"How many in your family?"

"There are seven of us. Three of us can work."

"What about the other four?" *Herr* Schmidt asked while lifting the paper revealing the creamy white block of cheese. The aroma instantly filled the space between them. Nick thought he could almost see the man salivating.

"My wife must care for my parents. They are elderly. And my daughter, Kati, is only 14. She will need to return to school."

"I see." *Herr* Schmidt sunk his teeth into the cheese that he had gingerly placed on top of the bread.

"You know, if you don't work, you don't eat. You will not get food rations for those in your family who do not work."

"*Ja*," Nick said. He didn't want to argue with *Herr* Schmidt.

"With all the rebuilding, we can easily find work for you as a carpenter. You will have to find your own transportation – it's across town."

"*Ja*, of course," Nick quickly agreed secretly wanting to hurry the arrangements along before *Herr* Schmidt finished his feasting.

"Your son can be useful there too, as an apprentice."

"Of course. And for my daughter, Leni?"

"There's a match factory not too far from the barracks where you will find housing. She can work there," *Herr* Schmidt said in a tone of finality and slight irritation. He carefully placed what remained of his sandwich down onto a cloth napkin as if it were made of glass. With one quick movement, he lifted a large round seal, stamped the papers, and signed them. Extending his right finger, he moved the documents across his desk.

"*Danke*," Nick said. He rose and offered his hand. *Herr* Schmidt immediately slid himself back into his chair, eyeing him with a sudden discomfort. For a moment, Nick was uncertain how to respond and then decided it was nothing more than a flaw in the man's character. He wasn't going to let anything interfere with the wonderful news he was about to bring home to his family.

Nick took a step forward, bent over, and picked up the papers that would change their lives. He nodded his head in thanks, pivoted on his right foot, and walked briskly through the open doorway from the man's office.

Once outside, Nick found himself walking quickly through the throngs of people. He had done it! Making his way over to the train station, he flew up the steps, grabbed the first available seat, and sat back against the wooden frame. He couldn't help smiling ear to ear. They were moving to Salzburg in the year 1947. Certainly, life was about to get better. He was sure of it.

Chapter Twenty-three

Nick slouched in the chair, tilting it back and forth on its hind legs. The autumn leaves were falling now. He felt uneasy thinking of the future and what it might hold for his family. Three years in Salzburg had passed quicker than he had realized and now another year was about to end.

Moving back into the barracks in 1947 wasn't as easy as it seemed, but Nick convinced his family it was for the best. When they first arrived in the refugee camp, Nick stood dumbfounded at the succession of buildings, one after another, after another. He counted 15 of them. It appeared before him like a small village. Inside the barracks, the tenants constructed temporary walls to divide up the allotted space among five families. Inside each family's unit, stood a simple stove, a few cabinets, and a large basin for washing. There was no running water, no sink, no bedrooms and no ice box. Privacy was scarce and brutally obvious when using the community bathrooms, one serving females the other for males.

The rudimentary living conditions had improved slightly when the family inherited more space, but the standard of living remained primitive. Food was rationed according to the number of working members in the family, and more times than not, it was difficult to stretch a meal. Europe was torn in two between the Soviet-occupied countries and the allies. The economy had undergone an assault. Famine was widespread and people did not believe recovery was coming any time soon.

Nick held onto his job as a cabinet maker but his oldest daughter, Leni, left her job at the match factory for one at a higher rate of pay at a custom box factory. Even though he disliked it, Nicky worked every day as a carpenter's apprentice. Kati, the youngest, picked up a cleaning job that included supper to ease the burden of another mouth to feed.

Old feelings of grief for having to leave Calma had turned into anger. Driven out to avoid Soviet occupation, the family was now considered displaced, or DPs, as some called them. Others accused them of being too lazy to stay in their village and help rebuild it, a ludicrous idea in Nick's opinion.

Nick sat still for a moment in his chair and let his mind wander back to the days in Calma. He wondered how it had changed since their departure. Surely, the Partisans had moved into their homes and enjoyed the fruits of their labors now. It was so unfair. Someone had referred to it as ethnic cleansing. Nick wasn't certain he understood what ethnic cleansing meant. All he knew was that they could never go home again. The desire for revenge on German citizens by Soviet-ruled countries, like Yugoslavia, meant suffering in concentration camps and slave labor. All rights of German citizens were revoked. All land ownership unrecognized. Those who remained behind became servants to the Partisans who now lived in their homes. It was heartbreaking. Facts and figures that made the news now identified 14-15 million ethnic Germans as displaced across central and Eastern Europe. The numbers were staggering and Nick and his family were part of it.

Nick shook his head from side to side, leaned forward, and placed his elbows on his thighs, lacing his fingers. *It wasn't all that bad here in Salzburg, was it?* They were enjoying the city life, each in their own way. The city was alive with festivals and dances. A simple stroll down the street admiring the little shops was enjoyable and romance bloomed for young couples behind the barracks in the evening. Nick certainly enjoyed his bowling nights and his children chatted endlessly about the Saturday night dances. But, little by little, the family began to give up hope; they began letting go of their dreams: the dreams they held for each other and for themselves. No longer did the future look promising, but instead, just as it was, one year after the next, after the next.

Nick thought about the talk that had been brewing among the men. Many families were signing up for visas and emigrating to the United Sates. If they couldn't get into the States, they went to Brazil, Canada, or Australia. They were going anywhere just to get out of the dismal life that held no hope for them in Germany or Austria. They left to make a new beginning. Nick remembered a conversation he had with Karl last week on bowling night.

"Nick, did you hear about that Displaced Persons Act America has?"

"What about it?"

"Well, we can get visas and go to America, that's

what! They're going to let hundreds of thousands of us in! But you have to be displaced, like us, unable to return home."

"*Ja*! My *fater* always said to go to America if I had the chance. What do you have to do to get a … what do you say, a visa?"

"You go to that Catholic center downtown and fill out a form. I went today."

"You did? You went today, Karl?"

"*Ja*. I hope we go to America! Have you ever asked yourself what we are doing here? We are dying here, Nick, and we don't even know it."

A crisp autumn breeze brought Nick back to the present moment. He rose to his feet so quickly it felt as if someone had spoken his name, bringing him out of the fog in which he found himself. The chair he had been sitting in tumbled sideways and fell to the ground. After remembering the conversation he had with Karl, the words of his father echoed in his mind over and over again, "*If you ever get the chance to go to America, go.*" The malaise Nick had been feeling earlier began to lift. He could feel his heart beating hard in his chest. He rolled up his shirt sleeves clear to his elbows. *Where are those certificates of birth?* In the passing of a moment, his future stood before him just as clear as the decision he had made to save his sweetheart so many years ago. He felt as if he stood at the brink of a crossroad. He had to gather his family. He had to tell them, and now, before it was too late. He only hoped it wasn't too late already.

Chapter Twenty-four

The lines at the National Catholic Welfare Conference (NCWC) stretched for at least a mile. People waited, looking at each other. They stood waiting for their futures, for opportunity, for escape. They shuffled their feet. Mothers moved their toddlers from hip to hip. Nick waited with them. He had his place in line. He heard the murmurs, the hushed tones. How America's streets were paved in gold and opportunity stood waiting for them.

Nick shuffled forward in the line being careful not to step on the heels of the couple ahead of him. He looked down at the certificates he held in his hand. Carl told him that was all he needed. There wasn't much left to bring anyway.

"Next."

Nick inched his way up to the large desk. A round pink face with warm brown eyes peered back at him. Her nametag read 'Mrs. Heinz' with the bold initials NCWC below it. She was smiling. It wasn't a smile that was forced but one that held promise and hope.

"May I help you?"

"I want to go to America." Nick blurted out while removing his cap.

"I see. Let's start with your name, shall we?" Mrs. Heinz motioned him to a nearby table. They walked side-by-side, not speaking. Nick could feel his anxiety building. He swallowed hard trying to ease his accelerating heartbeat. *What is she going to want to know? What if I don't have enough documentation? Will she ask me if I served Germany in the war? Will that disqualify my family?* So many questions bombarded Nick's mind that Mrs. Heinz had to repeat her offer for him to be seated. The chair she offered loomed ahead of him as if it held some type of mystical power that would force him to say too much or too little. He forced his feet forward and clumsily sat down, placing both of his arms on the worn, wooden armrests. He dug his fingers into the sleek, smooth edges causing a slight discomfort.

"Now, let's begin with your name and those of your family."

"My name is Nicholas Russ. There are seven in my family."

"Okay, Nicholas. May I call you Nicholas?"

"*Ja*, my friends call me, Nick."

"Okay," she repeated with a smile. "Nick. Do you understand what we do here at the National Catholic Welfare Conference?"

"I've been told that you are making out visas for people like us to go to America."

"That's correct. In 1948, President Truman passed something called The Displaced Persons Act allowing 205,000 emigrants to enter the United States."

"Why?"

"Why?" Mrs. Heinz repeated with a furrowed brow. "Well, Nick, I think the President wants to help. Think of it as a humanitarian effort for those who cannot return to their homeland."

Mrs. Heinz slid her forearms toward Nick closing the gap between them. Her kind smile and gentle voice calmed him almost instantly. She then entwined her fingers and placed her hands on top of the table.

"Are you afraid to go home, Nick?"

"Well, *Ja*, my country has been invaded by the Partisans and they are either killing us or sending us off to labor camps to die."

Mrs. Heinz lifted a clipboard. Nick could see a set of forms behind a thick metal clip.

"Nick, you will qualify for this program. All we have to do is complete this paperwork," she said firmly. "You will be issued International Red Cross passports and entry visas to the United States. You will board an American military ship in Germany returning to America after dropping off soldiers in Korea. It could take a while. You will need to be patient. And one more thing, Nick, you must take an oath to defend the United States with your life if you are called upon to do so. Will you agree to that?"

"*Ja*, I will agree."

"Nick, this will not be easy. Crossing the ocean in a military vessel will have its hardships. You'll need to prepare your family."

Nick nodded and looked back into the eyes of this kind stranger. Although he could not determine her age it was her warm brown eyes and soft chestnut hair that appealed to him the most because it reminded him of Theresa. He could feel the tension in his shoulder blades begin to release, as if Theresa was sitting right next to him. He rubbed his fingertips together and leaned forward placing his forearms on the desk. He was ready to get started on the most important journey of his lifetime, and he knew that Mrs. Heinz was going to help him get there.

As Mrs. Heinz flipped the pages recording the information for all seven of his family members, Nick divulged everything to her about his personal journey so far. It was as if the floodgates had opened, and he could finally release all that he was holding in - his conscription into the Yugoslav and German Armies, his duties in the war, Theresa's exodus from Calma, the end of the war and the journey to Austria and then on to Salzburg. He labored over the desperate times that were now part of their lives, times that held little hope without the option of simply going home to Calma and the good life they had there.

When they had finished their work together, Nick sincerely thanked her and then he bade Mrs. Heinz farewell. He felt drained, exhausted. As he made his way slowly out of the building, he looked around the large hall at the activity that surrounded him. Rows upon rows of patient people waiting for a second chance at life. People just like him, driven out of their homelands in order to keep their families safe. Where would they go? Where would they all end up? Australia? Brazil? Canada? Or, God willing, America, like Nick and his family. Nick continued his journey home knowing he had done everything he could to make this dream for his family come true. All he could do was wait.

Chapter Twenty-five

The news came on an ordinary day in October 1951. Nick rushed his steps, kicking the multicolored leaves in his path, crunching those that fell under foot. He could feel the excitement deep in his gut. It started after he read the letter. He held the envelope firmly in his hand careful not to impress it in any way. It was an important document, one that would set them free.

It had been nearly a month since his visit with Mrs. Heinz at the NCWC. She told him he would have to be patient. She said that getting the visas could take some time. But his family was beginning to give up hope as the days wore on. They persisted with their questions, and even Nick had allowed doubt to grow. It was his idea to move them to Salzburg, and now he felt responsible for getting them onto a ship and escaping a life that held no hope.

Nick turned the corner, facing the wind. He tucked his chin beneath his jacket and flipped up the collar. When he reached their barracks, he took the stairs two-by-two, pushed the heavy door open, quickly washed up for dinner in the lavatory and walked toward the unit they now called home. His mother's stern voice bellowed loudly through the thin walls, scolding his father to put down the newspaper. Nick smiled at the familiar banter and placed his hand securely around the door knob. The cool metal tingled against his skin. He swallowed thickly and waited a moment listening to the sounds of his family.

As he tightened his grip, he paused again realizing once he walked through that door, their lives would change forever. A surge of adrenaline kicked in. His heart responded with heavy thuds against his chest. Nick couldn't hold it in much longer. He turned the knob, opened the door, and stepped into the small room that acted as the living room, dining room, and bedroom.

Most of his family had taken their places at the kitchen table, expecting his arrival for dinner. Theresa and his mother were tending to supper, placing bowls of steaming vegetables, mashed potatoes, and chicken *paprikash* on the table. They both glanced up at him and smiled as he entered the room. His father folded the newspaper in half and tossed it onto a nearby chair. Leni, Kati, and Nicky were talking among themselves, as they often did, in an effort to amuse themselves and pass the time.

Nick slammed the door a bit more forcefully than he had intended. Everyone stopped what they were doing and looked at him. He spoke the words carefully but with the excitement of a child on Christmas morning.

"We...are...going...to...America!" he shouted while raising both his arms in a victory stance. He waved the envelope back and forth above his head. It felt so good to get out the words that he had been holding in since opening the letter. A roguish smile followed and splashed across his face. His eyes sparkled against the cast of the kitchen light. Leni and Kati immediately stood up, grabbed each other's hands, and began jumping up and down repeating, "America, America! We are going to be Americans!"

Nicky shook a firm fist in the air and smiled at his mother, then his grandparents. Theresa stood silent, pressing her palms against her cheeks. Her head shook back and forth as if she hadn't understood the words her husband had spoken.

"America!" Nick's father was the first to rise and walk toward him. The two exchanged bear hugs and Nick could feel the pride emanating from his father. "You did it, Nick," he said as he took a step back. He placed both of his hands on Nick's shoulders. "We are on our way to America!" Their glistening eyes locked. Looking into his father's eyes, Nick realized how desperate their situation really was, and what this trip meant to him.

"When do we leave *Datee*? When?" Leni was most anxious to quit her job at the box factory which had become duller with each day.

"What is this?" Nick asked in a teasing tone of voice, turning his attention to Leni. "What about your young man from Munich?" Nick was referring to a lukewarm romance between his oldest daughter and her recent beau that appeared to be going nowhere fast.

"Oh, *Datee,* you know that I would never stay behind alone." Nick laughed a hearty reply, knowing full well that Leni would always choose to be near her family.

"We leave on the first of November from Bremerhaven, Germany," Nick explained in a manner that sounded more like a tour guide than a father. With his heart rate beginning to slow down, he felt calmer and walked toward the kitchen table. He pulled out his chair and sat down. The rest of the family followed his lead, silently taking their seats, leaving their supper untouched for the moment. "We have passage on an American military ship that will be heading back to the United States." Nick said while making eye contact with each of his loved ones.

"What do you mean, Nick, when you say, 'back to the United States?'" Nick Sr. asked with an inquisitive look. His eyes stared straight ahead at Nick as he waited for his answer.

Nick leaned toward his father, giving him his full attention, "The Americans are dropping off soldiers in Korea to fight in the war." Nick felt a sense of pride to share this historical news with his father.

"Ah, ha," Nick's father's simple reply seemed to satisfy everyone who sat silent but aware of the lowered tones in conversation. "I've been listening to some of the men talk about that."

"A military ship, Nick?" Theresa interrupted the men with concern in her voice. Leni and Kati had stopped their whispering. "Yes, my darling. It will not be easy. We need to prepare ourselves for the journey. It could be rough at times."

"What should we expect?" Theresa asked.

Nick knew that Theresa's questions were more of a concern for their family than for herself. "We'll each have a bunk and some storage. If the weather cooperates, we can be on deck. Meals will be in the main dining room."

"And if we fall ill?" Theresa continued. Nick

knew Theresa was thinking of his mother who did not fare well with travel. He smiled at his wife respecting the empathy she had for others.

"There will be a doctor on board, but let's hope it doesn't come to that."

"I'm not sure I can do this, Nick," his mother blurted out, "I just don't have the strength." Nick thought his mother seemed to pale just thinking about the trip. Her eyes darted away from his. She leaned back into her chair, wrapping her arms snugly around her waist. She always had a sensitive stomach, and Nick feared the trip across the Atlantic Ocean would take its toll on her.

"We'll all be there, Eva," Nick's father interjected, as he touched his wife's shoulder. "You will not be alone. We'll take good care of you." Nick knew his father's soothing words and tender touch were meant to console his mother, who attempted a smile, but made her point very clear with her eyes.

"How long, *Datee*, how long until we are Americans?" Kati asked, breaking the solemn feel the room had suddenly fallen under. She drummed her fingers across the kitchen table as if she were pressed for time.

"Well, I don't know that, Katarina," Nick replied, thankful to be smiling again. "We must first get across the water, okay?"

Nick gazed at Kati, his fair-haired daughter. Since she was not comfortable with change, Nick was suddenly concerned that this journey would be a test of strength for her. Kati was not like Leni, who was strong-willed and forceful when necessary. Nick couldn't count the number of times he was grateful for Leni, the one he could depend on to lead the others.

"Do we land in New York?" Nick's father asked, pulling Nick out of his own reverie and back to the conversation.

"*Ja*. We stop at Ellis Island to be processed. Then, we wait in New York for our sponsor."

Nick's father nodded. "I've gone through the Island years ago when working in the States."

Across the table, Nicky swiped a finger full of mashed potatoes. Theresa immediately scolded him and attempted to slap the top of his hand. The boy inched back into the safety of his chair.

"Tsk," Nick's mother's face squiggled into an unfavorable glance.

"What will we do in New York, *Datee*?" Nicky asked, trying to regain the good graces he had just lost.

"We wait. I know the sponsor is a farmer, but that's about it. He'll need to complete some paperwork, accepting responsibility for us. In exchange, we will work for him for a year."

"Doing what, Nick?" Theresa had been silent for a while, but her concern resurfaced.

"I don't know what." Nick hoped he didn't sound as irritated as he was beginning to feel. The questions were beginning to mount and his nerves suddenly felt frayed. It had been a long day and his body was beginning to feel it.

"We will find that out when we meet him," Nick said.

"They pick us up like baggage – eh?" Nick's father said under his breath while rubbing the stubble on his chin. Nick's mother placed her hand on his father's forearm but said nothing.

Nick felt his defenses rise. He had gone to a lot of trouble to get these visas, yet little by little, the questions were beginning to leave him with a sense of disapproval.

"We will be lucky to find someone who will take in seven strangers who are unable to speak their language."

Nick could feel the hairs on the back of his neck rise. "God bless them." His voice grew in intensity. "And I don't even know them yet!" Nick slapped his hand on top of the kitchen table, causing the dishes and silverware to rattle against each other.

"They are getting a good deal too, Nick," his father said as he stood up from his place at the table. He raised his hand toward Nick. Pressing his fingers against his thumb, he went on, face reddened. "Cheap, cheap labor from people who know how to put in a day's work. Don't forget about that."

After a moment, he sat back down in his seat and shuffled his chair toward the table. Nick looked around the table, but all eyes were downcast. The room fell silent as the two men regained their composure.

"*Ja*," Nick replied, nodding his head in agreement. He had experienced enough excitement for one night. He picked up the bowl of mashed potatoes, plopped a hearty scoop onto his plate, and the family began their dinner.

Chapter Twenty-six

To Nick, the next month felt like a year. Finally, the day to leave Salzburg had arrived. Standing at the port in Bremerhaven with his family, he looked down at the wooden boxes he had built for each one of them. For a moment, he was overcome with sadness that a lifetime of belongings could be contained in a simple box. *Was that all we have acquired in life?* Nick chased the negative thought from his mind. Their situation was about to change, dramatically. He looked down at the visas he held in his hand and squeezed. He hoped that America truly was a place where dreams come true, even for a boatload of poor emigrants.

Nick took notice of the people who surrounded him. He wondered if their stories were similar to his. He stood next to his father, who seemed to be enjoying all the activity. Theresa was directly behind them, laughing and talking with Kati, Leni, and Nicky. Nick's mother, Eva, stood stiffly next to Theresa.

Nick let out a sigh of relief. With the exception of his mother, his family seemed to be in good spirits, at least for now. After the barrage of questions and concerns he had fielded for the last several weeks, he was second guessing if the trip was a good idea.

"So, we're really going to do this!" his father

said, beaming. He lightly slapped Nick's back. Out of all them, Nick's father seemed to be the most excited.

"That's right," Nick replied, wearing a thin smile.

"What's bothering you, Nick?" His father turned to face him.

"Just thinking of Helen and Josef staying behind in Munich."

"Your sister will be just fine." Nick's father said.

Nick was struggling with Helen's decision to remain in Munich but understood her reasons. Her daughter-in-law, Lisie, didn't want to leave her parents. And Helen and Josef couldn't leave Lisie and their son. So, the decision was made to remain in Munich and make a life.

"You can't blame Lisie or Helen," Nick's father said.

"I'm not blaming anyone." In an instant, Nick felt like a child. "It's just hard to leave them behind," Nick said in a flat tone.

"We'll come back. We'll visit." Nick knew his father was trying to neutralize his feelings. He was good at that, listening and keeping peace in the family. Why hadn't Nick ever realized that?

"*Ja*, maybe." Nick agreed, but privately doubted if that would ever happen. "I'll be glad to get on board." Nick smiled at his father, hoping to change the subject.

When they reached the gangplank, Nick stared at the young man accepting the visas.

"Navy man," his father said.

Nick nodded a silent yes.

A young man with sandy brown hair extended his hand to accept the visas. Nick quickly turned them over to him and noticed the fine uniform he was wearing a dark navy blue wool with thick white stripes on the sleeves. Nick turned his head to catch a glimpse of an eagle that was stitched onto the left sleeve with some bars beneath it. He was certain that it signified a rank the young man had earned. Nick nodded his head with a curt smile the officer's way. He motioned them aboard.

Once on deck, Leni, Kati, and Nicky disappeared in the excitement of discovery. Nick and Theresa stood side-by-side with his parents and the foursome watched as the remaining passengers boarded, surprised to recognize a few of them from the camp.

Nick could feel his stomach reacting to the excitement, fear, and anticipation of what was to come. He knew the butterflies in his stomach were signaling him to run. But run where? This is what he wanted, to go to America, even as an uneasy feeling passed through him from head to toe. It was one thing to move from one village to another across Europe; however, sailing across the Atlantic Ocean in a military cruiser felt a whole lot different. He silently rifled through the fears that were beginning to mount in his mind: the journey over the Atlantic; arriving in New York; the sponsor and their home for the next year; learning a new language; supporting his family.

It was all so overwhelming.

Nick sucked the crisp autumn air deep into his lungs, squaring up his shoulders. He slipped his hand into Theresa's and pulled her closer. Her soft brown eyes looked into his. Nick sensed that she intuitively knew his struggle. A genuine smile lit up her face and in that moment, everything became clear. He brushed her lips softly with his own and knew that whatever came their way, they would make it. As the ship pulled away from the dock, Nick took a long look at the shoreline of his home country and bade farewell.

"*Auf Wiedersehen,*" he whispered, unsure of when he would ever set eyes on it again.

Chapter Twenty-seven

The voyage started out at a pleasant pace. Most days, the adult passengers spent the afternoons comparing stories and playing cards. Nick was interested in how many of them shared the conviction that traveling across the ocean was the only option. It amazed him how many people were truly suffering.

"Theresa, would you like to take a stroll around the deck?" Nick asked, wearing a sheepish grin. She still moved him, even after 21 years.

"I'd love to," Theresa replied, swiveling her gaze in the direction of her coat.

Nick looked forward to their nightly walks after supper. It helped pass the time while giving him a stolen moment alone with his wife.

"Your mother has started complaining already," Theresa said. "She told me earlier that, 'the boat is bobbing around like a cork in the water.'"

Nick chuckled. "Yes, she's not one to hold her opinion to herself, is she? If she's complaining that's a good sign, that means she's still feeling okay."

"It's hard not to admire this mighty ship."

"*Ja*, sometimes, I find myself just listening to the sounds that it makes."

Nick enclosed Theresa's hand in his as they made

their way around the deck a second time. He was feeling better than he had in weeks now that the trip was underway. Many times he felt the butterflies of excitement tingling in his stomach.

"Did you notice how everyone is acting as if this trip to New York is just a short boat ride across a lake?" Nick asked.

Theresa nodded. "Today, Adala said she heard it may not take as long as we all thought; that we could arrive before than the 12th."

"What is she thinking?" Nick asked, now irritated. "We haven't even cleared the English Channel yet. *Fater* said it will be at least 11 days and maybe more if we run into bad weather."

"Oh, I hope we don't run into storms, Nick. I'm afraid the children will end up with seasickness. Leni has already been complaining of an upset stomach."

"Leni has?"

Theresa nodded. Nick knew that if Leni became ill the others were sure to follow. His father had told him to expect rougher passage once they were out in the open ocean. Nick swallowed hard, fearing what was waiting for them in the days to come.

As predicted, when the ship cleared the English Channel and hit the open ocean, things began to change, rapidly. A few travelers complained of seasickness, then a few more. By midweek, Nick and his entire family were suffering from the illness and Eva was among the very ill, refusing to eat.

They spent their days lying on their bunks, rising only to run to the latrine. Most times, they would make it, vomiting profusely. Other times, they would not. The stench that built up below deck was nearly intolerable but the most difficult to bear were the storms that crept in and raised havoc. Nick started picking up on the body language as he watched the crew interpret the warning signs in the darkened clouds and violent winds. They would motion with their arms and order everyone below deck. The hatches would be sealed as life vests and flashlights were distributed. Meanwhile, passengers clung to their bunks to wait out the storm.

As the waves crested over the boat, smashing onto the stern, it sounded to Nick as if the boat had collided with a sea of rocks, but it was only the angry sea howling the dreadful, deadly sounds. To calm their children, Nick and Theresa would gather them together and talk about the new life that awaited them. They spoke of their new dreams and how fortunate they were to be on the ship heading for America.

As they drifted into the week's end, they all began to feel much better and the days had become more tolerable. People were beginning to re-emerge from below and the conversations began once again. One of the exceptions was Eva, who was still gravely ill. With the beginning of each new day, the family feared it would be her last. The last time she ate was the day of their departure and the family was drained from the illness themselves. Each night they spent more and more time with her before turning in, fearing she would not see the light of day.

"Give me some bread with onions!" Eva shouted.

Nick rose with a start to hear his mother yelling. *What time is it?* He felt disoriented. For a moment, Nick wondered if the ship had stopped, but he soon realized it was gliding across the water, at a quick pace. He quickly slipped on his robe and shoes and hastened his steps. One by one, the rest of the family rose and gathered at Eva's bed to hear the words they were praying to hear.

"I'm so hungry," she croaked.

"What would you like to eat, Mother?" Theresa asked while appearing to be ready to bolt in a moment's notice. Bending over Eva, she carefully had her sip on some water.

"Bread and raw onions," Eva said between sips.

"I'll run to the kitchen." Handing the glass to Leni, Theresa was off in a flash, her robe billowing behind her.

"Well, it's about time, Eva." Her husband said, shuffling over to her bedside. A mischievous smile spread across his face. His arms were folded, resting on his chest. "We thought you were about done in," he smirked.

"Done in!" Eva shrieked. Kati and Leni took a step back, startled at their grandmother's protest. "I was just a little under the weather, that's all. What day is it?"

"Mother," Nick said bending down near her bunk, "It's Sunday. You've been sick all week. We all were so worried."

Eva looked into eyes of her son and smiled. "I'm okay now, Nick, I'm going to be alright." Her hand reached up to touch the side of his face. Now's where's my bread?" she asked, looking for Theresa.

November 12th was a day like no other. Nick and Theresa stood on the deck, both holding tightly onto the cold, metal railing. Bundled up in their winter coats, they stood in silence, forcing the crisp, fresh air to clear their lungs of the staleness from below. They could hear their children off in the distance but not too far from them. They gazed out into the water oblivious to the fact that they were entering New York Harbor. Nick was deep in thought, something that had happened quite frequently to him since boarding the ship. They passed Coney Island and traveled between Brooklyn and Staten Island when out of nowhere, the boat's horn began to blow a deep blare, startling both of them. Theresa placed her hand on Nick's arm. But it was the commotion taking place on the bow that caught his attention.

"Nick! Nick!" His father's voice bellowed out from somewhere in the distance. "Come here! You've got to see this!" Nick could see his father's head bobbing in search of him between the passengers heading in his direction.

"Theresa, stay close to me," Nick said. Squeezing her hand tightly within his, he began sidestepping the others, heading in the direction of his father's voice. Those ahead of him began clapping and screaming. Some people were crying. *What was going on?* Nick could see Leni, Kati, and Nicky running alongside of him, their jackets flapping in the wind.

"Here, Nick, get closer," his father urged.

"It's magnificent," he heard his mother say. She was standing nearby, her mouth slightly opened, as she stared at the Statue of Liberty. It had been a long time since Nick had seen his mother so impressed with something that it took her breath away.

"Are we in America now?" Nicky asked his

grandmother.

"Yes, Nicky, we are."

"Do you see her, Nick?" His father's gaze was fixed straight ahead. The cold November wind slapped against their faces causing a sting, but no one seemed affected. Despite the weather, they all would have chosen to be standing right where they were at this very moment to witness a passage that would change their lives forever.

Nick followed his father's gaze to the iridescent green figure standing proudly on a pedestal, rising up from the water. Nick guessed it had to be 1,500 kilometers in the air. She wore a spiked crown. Her thick right arm was extending into the sky and in it she held a torch. The other arm was folded, holding a tablet.

"A lady. A beautiful lady," Kati shrieked.

"Look at her, *Datee*. She's so lovely." Leni said standing near him now.

"Lady Liberty," Nick's father murmured as if greeting an old friend. "She's freedom, Nick. You now have the freedom to do whatever you want to do and live wherever you want to live."

"America! America!" Those around Nick began to chant, softly. They hugged and kissed and spoke softly to each other as they ferried closer and closer to the magnificent statue. Nick stood mesmerized by the gravity of what he was seeing. He no longer heard his father's voice or those around him. The regal statue stood firmly in front of a backdrop of automobile lights flickering behind her. For the first time in his life, Nick was at a loss for words.

Nick felt Theresa behind him and maneuvered her

in front of him. He wrapped his arms around her waist. She gasped at the scene unfolding in front of her, the beautiful lady who would give them a new life.

As the ship entered the Hudson River, an endless stream of automobile lights darted in all directions. It was an amazing sight for Nick and his family. No one owned a car in Calma.

"Look at the autos," shrieked Kati standing near her parents, "so many of them, one after another!"

"Yes, sweetheart," Theresa replied, "it's ... amazing."

Nick snuggled closer to Theresa. "We're home, Theresa," Nick whispered as he nibbled on her ear lobe.

Nick could tell Theresa was just as moved as he. She laid her head back onto his shoulder, repeating his words, "home."

Nick and his family waited impatiently as they slowly progressed in line to disembark. They were told to wait on the pier for the ferry that would take them to the island. The sight before them was a little intimidating. The progression of buildings on Ellis Island appeared worn and tired. Nick surmised that 50 years of cataloging emigrants would do that to a building. He had heard in conversation that more than 10 million emigrants had passed through this island. The number was staggering and Nick couldn't really imagine it. At the same time, he realized after today, he and his family would be included in that number.

Once on shore, Nick heard a man directing the passengers to find their luggage in the baggage area. Nick and his father led the family by following those in front of them to a pile of bags, bundles, and boxes that people had been sifting through. And then Nick saw them.

"Over here," Nick said now grateful for the unique boxes he had made for his family. They sat in plain sight just a few yards away, stacked one on top of the other. Nicky ran ahead and began distributing each one to correct family member.

After gathering up their luggage, they made their way up the stairs to the Great Hall. Before leaving the ship, Nick had briefed his family to take the stairs at a consistent pace, to look strong and able-bodied and even laugh, pretending it was a social event. He was told from some of the deck hands that they would be observed for physical ailments as they climbed the staircase and Nick didn't want anything to go wrong now. He learned of stories where emigrants were sent back to their native land because of a serious crime or a contagious disease and began understanding why the island got its name, *Land of Tears*.

Nick looked behind him at the ocean in the distance and the sea of people surrounding him. With each step, his anticipation grew. When he reached the top, he was sure that this moment was probably one of the most exciting times of his life.

"Keep the lines moving, keep moving forward." A man dressed in a crisp blue-grey uniform motioned his arms to help communicate the command. He spoke both English and German. Nick admired the round brass buttons that held the man's jacket closed. His round cap bobbed up and down as he spoke. The officer looked at Nick and opened his hand as if expecting something.

"Documents, please," he commanded. Nick placed the seven visas into his hand and waited as he rifled through them. He fastened a tag onto Nick's coat, and pointed him in the direction of a long line beneath a sign that read, *Registry Room.*

"This way," Nick said, motioning to his family.

"Where must we go, Nick?" Theresa asked. Nick knew Theresa wanted this process to go quickly. She had admitted to him that she was concerned for Leni, Kati, and Nicky, as well as his parents. It had been a long, draining trip and nerves were on edge.

"We need to register over there," he pointed across the room.

As they walked through the common area in the Great Hall, Nick felt as if he were walking into complete mayhem. Cattle grid segregated passengers in long lines. *This could take hours*, mentally complaining to himself now sharing Theresa's concern. He noticed children crying while others played. He saw a few people lying on benches sound asleep, while others sat alone in utter silence. Women wearing colored babushkas passed them by heading in another direction. Old men with long beards stared at them. Boxes, crates, and bundles in piles cluttered adjacent walkways. It was chaotic and not what Nick had expected.

He was uncertain what he expected when they landed and disembarked from the ship. An extraordinary amount of excitement carried them from the Statue of Liberty to the Great Hall at Ellis Island. But now that they were inside the building, exhilaration had faded and confusion was beginning to settle in.

"Look at the children, Mother," Leni said.

"Yes, I see them, Leni," Theresa replied with a firm undertone, "keep walking; follow *Datee*."

"But why are they crying?"

"Magdalena, follow *Datee!*" Theresa commanded.

Nick and his family marched across the Great Hall sticking close together. They each carried their boxes close at their sides. When they reached their destination Nick instructed them to wait on the benches nearby while he took his place in line. When they had arrived, they were handed a small amount of food to share among them. Now, thankful for the piece of bread that he had stowed away, he removed it from his pocket, tore off a good-sized piece and jammed it into his mouth. He hoped by eating it, he would feel better and the dizziness would pass. He was uncertain why he felt this way; the last few days on board had gone so well.

When it was finally his turn in line, he was asked for his visas and birth certificates. After answering a series of questions including his name, those in his family, and the money he carried with him among others, he was pointed in another direction under a huge sign that read *Physicals*. He turned now and faced his family. They looked tired as they sat waiting, faces drained. Nick wished he could somehow hurry this process along but he felt helpless. *This was the way it was to be and they just had to be strong for a little while longer.*

Chapter Twenty-eight

Nick gathered up his family and escorted them over to the next line. He stepped forward to reach the attendant behind the desk. His family followed, creating a halo effect around him.

"Females this way," the attendant shouted, "and males that way." She pointed in two opposite directions. Nick nodded to her, but raised his hand, as if to ask for a moment. He turned now to address his family, wondering how he would explain this next step. Placing one hand on Leni and the other on Nicky, he drew them together in a huddle. He took a breath and knew if he remained calm, they would too.

"The next thing we must do is a physical examination."

"What!" Leni gasped in horror, placing her hand on her chest. Kati immediately clutched her sister's other hand and gulped hard. Theresa took a step forward closing the gap between her and the girls.

"Don't worry girls," Theresa said and placed a hand on each one of their shoulders. "I'll be with you. We'll go together."

"Can we, *Datee?* Can we stay together as mama says?" Kati asked, her eyes widening.

"Yes, Kati." Nick said, calmly. "All the girls will

go together and the men will do the same. We'll meet right back here when we're finished. They want to check our eyes, ears, and hair."

"What are they looking for?" Nicky asked his father. He stood proud and unafraid, unlike his sisters.

"Lice and bad diseases like TB."

"What happens if you have TB?" Nicky prodded. His eyebrows shot up.

"You get sent back. They won't let you into the United States."

Theresa put her hand over her mouth to muffle her protest while the rest of the family stared back with wide eyes and frightened looks.

"What about my illness on the ship? What if they find out about that?" Eva sputtered, clearly concerned.

"They are not looking for that, Mother," Nick reassured her, "but for other things." He didn't want to alarm his mother with what he had heard on the ship yesterday – that anyone displaying any type of illness would be subject to more than just a physical, held in the hospital facility, or simply sent back. He would bear that worry himself.

Unlike the rest of his family, his father looked as if he were in a *gasthaus* waiting for a stein of beer. Nick thought about his father's visits to America from years past and assumed it was helping him now cope with this chaos.

Nick turned forward, inching them toward the segregated lines. He paused, wondering how his father made the trip to America over and over, all alone, staying years at a time. He understood *why* he did it: so they could have better life back in Calma. But *how* could he do it? Nick shook his head. He couldn't imagine making this journey even once more.

A special camaraderie with his father began to grow deep inside of Nick. Wasn't he embracing the very same challenge, only decades later? He was following in his father's footsteps to America to create a better life for his family. Nick looked over his shoulder meeting his father's gaze. He smiled, not a wide-grin but one he hoped would communicate the increased respect and admiration he now felt for his father.

"We're going to make it, Nick." His father said as he followed Nick into the physical examination area and nodded his head as if to reaffirm his statement. Nicky followed behind the two older men. Nick nodded back, feeling at a loss for the right words. But, true to his father's prediction, less than an hour later, the family found each other in the common area again, having passed their physicals without a problem.

"There's one more thing I need to do before we can leave," Nick explained to his family.

"What next, *Datee*? I'm so hungry, and it's dirty in here." Kati scowled. Her eyes drifted over her surroundings.

"I know, Katrina, just be patient. I need to go over to there." Nick sat down next to Kati on the bench, squiggling in between her and Nicky. He wanted to take a few minutes to explain to the children what was happening. It had been a long and confusing day for them. He pointed across the room to an area marked *Red Cross Catholic Aid*. It would be the last stop for the day.

"What are you going to tell them, Nick?" Theresa asked, her brow furrowed as she spoke.

"I'm going to make arrangements to pay them back for our passage once we start working. Remember, that's what they told me to do at the NCWC?" Nick nodded while speaking, trying to jog Theresa's memory.

Although she didn't reply, Theresa nodded, and then took a seat next to Eva.

Nick knew she was beginning to tire, as were his parents who were awfully quiet these last couple of hours. The three of them sat together on the bench with drawn-out faces. His father toyed with his feet, tapping one against the other.

"What do they want from you, *Fater?*" Nicky asked, gesturing toward the aid desk.

Nick turned his focus on his children, who sat on the opposite side of the bench hoping to simplify a delicate matter.

"They want to know that we will stand behind our word and pay them back for our trip."

"We have no money to pay now?" Leni asked, boldly. Now 19, Leni had grown up. She and Nick shared many conversations lately concerning the world and how things operated financially.

"What little we have, I want to hold on to. We will work for our sponsor. He will pay us wages. Then we will make payments to the Red Cross for our voyage." Nick pointed again to the Catholic aid area. "It's a small price to pay for coming to America, right?" Nick tapped the knees of all three of his children, who returned a smile back to him.

"Right, *Datee,*" they replied simultaneously.

"Okay, I won't be long then." Nick stood, walked over to Theresa, bent down and kissed her on the cheek.

Her lips curled up at the corners. Turning on the balls of his feet, he walked swiftly across the room, feeling six sets of eyes following him.

Chapter Twenty-Nine

Standing in line, Nick thrust his fists into his pockets, as if searching for money that he knew he would not find. He hated this feeling. Not once had he ever borrowed money from anyone. Nevertheless, he forced his shoulders back and head up and vowed it would be the last time he would ever let himself feel this way again.

"The fee is $149 a person," a stout, middle-aged man spoke to Nick in German.

"How many in your family?" he asked.

"Seven," Nick replied.

"Are you prepared to pay for passage today or through the sponsor program?"

"The sponsor program." Nick said quickly, as if the words held a bitter taste on his tongue.

"I see," the attendant replied. He gathered up a few documents, looked up at Nick and said, "come with me."

Nick followed him over to a brown wooden table where he was handed the paperwork and a ballpoint pen.

"You will need to fill out this form listing your family members." He shuffled the first aside and pointed to the next. "This one is for the repayment option. When you sign these documents, you are agreeing to reimburse the Red Cross for your passage. The repayment starts immediately."

"Where do I send the payments?" Nick asked. His eyes scanned over the document looking for the information.

"Right here." The attendant's thick finger pointed to an address along with mailing instructions. "There's a carbon copy for your records. Is this something you are willing to agree to?"

Nick nodded, but wondered what if he had said no. Would they return his family to Germany? He wasn't aware of any other alternative. He brushed the thoughts from his mind, blaming them on exhaustion. He pulled out the chair and sat down.

"What about our sponsor?" Nick scolded himself for almost forgetting to ask the most important question.

"We will send word as soon as we know who it is." The attendant smiled and patted Nick's shoulder as if to console him. "You'll be staying at a hotel nearby. Can we split up your family to multiple sponsors?"

"No, it's important we stay together," Nick was quick to answer.

"Well, it may take up to a week, since you all want to stay together. We'll do our best."

"Thank you," Nick said with a tone of genuine gratitude. He picked up the pen and began filling in the form, grateful to see it was written in German. When he was finished, Nick returned the completed documents to the attendant. Nick watched as the stout little man ripped and tore the documents at the perforated seams with seasoned hands and placed them in an envelope.

"Welcome to America, Mr. Russ." The attendant placed the packet in his hand that contained his copies.

"Thank you," Nick sputtered.

As the packet rested in his hand, Nick realized it was finally over: obtaining the visas, leaving Germany, the voyage, and finally completing the naturalization process. Nick rushed back across the hall to his family with a sprint in his step, dodging through the newcomers just arriving. The exhilaration had reappeared, the excitement brewing.

"Let's go everyone," he urged when he saw them, clapping his hands in excitement. "We are all done."

Kati was the first one to leap from the bench and follow alongside her father, the others trailing behind them as they made their way outside.

Nick filled his lungs with the crisp November air. It felt good to be out of the building and outside again. He stood at the top of the stairs and paused a moment, watching his children now ahead of him. *Their futures will be in America,* he thought. A surge of happiness spread deep inside of him. He shivered, wondering if it was the weather or the sudden realization that they were on their way to becoming Americans.

"Where do we go from here?" Nick's father asked, closing the space between them. Theresa and Eva followed silently behind the two men.

Nick pointed toward the cars parked in the street below.

"The volunteers will be driving us to a hotel nearby. Then, we wait until the Red Cross matches us up with a sponsor." Nick began descending the stairs. "Because we are a large family, it could take a while."

"A while? How long is that?" Theresa interrupted. She and Eva had been keeping pace with the men listening to their every word as they made their way down the stairs.

Nick winced, hoping to avoid Theresa's barrage of questions. It had been a long day.

"Nick!" She repeated, her voice laced with irritation. "How long?"

"A couple of weeks, maybe less." Nick answered but knew the vague remark would not go unnoticed.

"What will we do for a couple of weeks?" she persisted.

"Discover our new surroundings," Nick's father said with a grin. Nick was thankful for his father's intervention.

Nick glanced at Theresa and winked. "Everything's going to work out, Theresa. You'll see," he said. "We stay put in the hotel until we know who our sponsors are." Nick didn't want to lose the momentum he had been feeling. "Let's enjoy our new home country." He waved his hand as if to present New York especially to her.

Twilight was upon them and the city was coming alive before their eyes in a spectacular showcase of lights that they had never seen before.

"This is so exciting. Look at the city. The lights!" Nicky said.

"*Ja*, Nicky," Nick said, grateful for the infusion of the boy's enthusiasm. Nick grabbed him in a loose hug. "What a magnificent night!" he added.

After a brief introduction to the drivers, the family helped load their wooden suitcases into the trunks of the cars, and took their seats inside the two vehicles. Nick sat back against the cushion. An exhausted sigh escaped him. He crossed his arms and smiled. It was over.

Chapter Thirty

As the Red Cross predicted, Nick and his family waited almost three weeks before hearing word that Hank and Mabel White, from Kingston, North Carolina, had signed on as their sponsors. Nick learned that the Whites were farmers who grew tobacco. They had sponsored many emigrants in years past. Nick didn't waste any time getting their release papers processed. He marched right over to the train depot and booked passage. They would arrive in nearby Goldsboro, located in the coastal plains region of the state. The Red Cross would arrange for Hank and Mabel to meet them at a station.

"What do any of us know about tobacco farming?" Nick's father asked him before turning in for the night. It had been a stressful couple of weeks and nerves were on edge.

"Nothing," Nick admitted, "but we can learn. I figure you, me, and Kati will work the farm. Hopefully, Leni, Theresa, and Nicky can find jobs. And Mama will run the house."

"*Ja,*" Nick's father replied, but Nick noticed a look of concern in his eyes.

"It's only for a year, and then we can move on and do whatever we want to do with the rest of our lives."

"I'm 73 years old, Nick. I'm not sure how much more I can do."

Nick glanced at his father understanding exactly what he was trying to say. "I need your advice more than anything else, to help me figure out how to make this next year work."

Nick slouched forward and rested his forehead against his fingertips. He was beginning to feel the stress build in the back of his neck.

Nick's father laid a gentle hand on Nick's back. "We're going to make it, Nick."

It was a cold day in December when they all climbed aboard the train heading to North Carolina. Everyone was eager to leave the small one-room hotel room they all had to share. Nick was the first to board the train, but before he boarded, he noticed how the black Americans were steered toward a different train car than their own. A quizzical look flitted across his face.

"*Datee?*" Leni whispered in his ear, "What is going on here?"

Before he could answer her, he felt Kati tugging on the opposite coat sleeve and suspected she too felt uneasy. Nick shook his head to discourage any further questions from either of the girls. He scanned the train car quickly and selected the first bank of seats, near the front.

"It's segregation," said Nick's father. He had followed close behind the girls and overheard Leni's question. "It's common here in the United States. I remember it from years ago. Apparently, things haven't changed much."

"What is segregation?" Nicky asked his grandfather, quickly taking a seat next to his elder.

"Well, the Jim Crow laws separate the coloreds from the whites." Nick's father explained.

"The coloreds?" Leni asked.

"The black people, Leni," her grandfather answered.

Why do they want to separate them?" Kati asked with a quizzical look.

"At first, the law was meant to protect them."

"Is this the only Crow law in America?" Nicky asked. "That the coloreds have to ride in separate cars on the train?"

Nick curled around in his seat and listened to the conversation.

"No. There are all kinds of laws they must follow."

"Like what?" Nicky asked so quickly, Nick's father could barely take in his next breath.

"Well," he answered as he exhaled, "Any time they want to use public transportation, like a train, a bus, or a ferry boat, they must ride in a separate car, like we've seen today, or take a seat in the back."

"That's silly," Kati said.

Nick noticed that not only were his children listening attentively to his father but his wife and mother as well. He snickered to himself, knowing his father was enjoying this moment.

"Is that it?" Leni asked.

"No. There are restaurants, drinking fountains, and separate schools for their children too. Now, there are some businesses that flat out refuse to serve them."

Leni shook her head in silent disbelief.

"That doesn't make any sense," Nicky said.

"Well, that's what we might think, but the Americans do not. This has been the law for a very long time and it doesn't look like it's about to change any time soon."

"I've never seen a black person before," Leni whispered across the aisle, hoping to reach her grandfather's ears but no one else's.

"Me either," said Kati, crossing her arms at her waist.

"I know," said Nick's father.

Nick had seen a few black Americans during the war, but he knew his family had not. He wasn't about to explain the issue of segregation beyond what his father had offered. It was just something his family would have to get used to.

Once the train started moving, Nick changed the subject by pointing out the changing landscape. A whole new world was unfolding right before their eyes. As the big city lights of the East faded away, rolling hills of the South took their place. Rich farmland unrolled while the train meandered toward its destination, tobacco country.

As Nick continued to watch the scenic view, he thought about the coming year and knew he would miss working as a carpenter. But he and his family had to learn a whole new language, and he was counting on the White family to help them.

Chapter Thirty-one

Before he knew it, Nick could feel the train beginning to slow. As they pulled into the station, Theresa tapped him on the shoulder from her seat behind him and pointed out how the wind appeared to be toying with the moss that hung from the cypress trees. Nick watched as her eyes followed the dancing movement of the moss and he smiled. She still captivated him even though they celebrated their twenty-first wedding anniversary a couple of weeks ago.

"Are we here, *Datee*? Kati asked when the train finally stopped.

"Looks like we are," Nick replied but quickly added, "Katarina, stay close now. Don't wander off."

Nick and his family rose to their feet and stepped down onto the depot platform. They followed the other travelers and retrieved their luggage. Nick looked around and felt a little unsettled. He didn't know where to lead his family or what Hank White looked like. He felt vulnerable and didn't like it.

"Let's stand over here." Nick pointed to a less crowded area a few yards from where they were huddled together.

"Are you sure you'll be able to find him there?" Eva asked. Her concern rising.

"*Ja*, let's go," Nick ordered.

"What are we doing, Nick?" Theresa asked.

As Nick led the group to the side, he could sense the escalating irritability in their questions.

"We are going to wait out this mayhem. The last thing I need is for one of us to get lost in a place where no one knows our language!" His voice was firm and disinvited further discussion.

Nick could feel his patience running thin. He scanned the crowd, trying to locate Hank, but could feel his own frustration beginning to fester. He had no idea how he'd ever find him in this chaos.

"*Datee*? Where is he?" Nicky asked.

Nick knew that Nicky was referring to the sponsor and fought the urge to snap at the boy.

"Well, I don't know yet." Nick said trying to remain calm. "There are too many people to sift through. I don't even know who I'm looking for."

"Well," his father said, "we know he's middle-aged, about 50 years old, right?"

Nick knew, once again, his father was trying to smooth things over and keep him calm.

"*Ja*." Nick said. "His wife may be with him." he added.

The family stood huddled together, watching the activity around them. Ten minutes had passed but to Nick it felt more like thirty. Finally, the crowd cleared.

"Is that him?" Eva pointed toward a gentleman who appeared to be scanning the crowd just a few yards away. He was dressed in a pair of light cotton slacks, a plaid shirt, and leather jacket. A thin veil of dust lined his boots. His face was weathered from years of working in the sun. He held an envelope in his hand.

Nick snapped his head in his mother's direction. His eyes met up with the stranger's. Trusting his instincts, Nick took a few steps toward him, the family following his every move. The man did the same thing, at almost the same time. A smile broke out between them, and they both quickened their steps toward each other. When they reached one another, they shook hands, a custom Nick was beginning to use more and more since arriving to America.

"Mr. Russ?" The man asked.

"*Ja,*" Nick replied, recognizing his Americanized pronounced name and nodded.

"Hank White," he said slowly.

Feeling inept in his ability to communicate, Nick's cheeks flushed in embarrassment. From the envelope he was holding, Hank pulled out a document, and Nick noticed the familiar logo at the top. Nick looked at the document but could only make out his name since it was written in English. Once again, trusting his instincts, he nodded at Hank to convey he understood that they had found each other.

Nick could feel Theresa standing behind him. He reached for her and gently pulled her toward him.

Hank gestured to Nick and his family to follow him. He raised his arms in front of him, clutching an imaginary wheel, imitating driving.

"Let's follow him," Nick instructed his family. "I think he wants to lead us to his automobile."

They wandered across a small parking lot, weaving around the few cars and trucks that remained. Even though the parking lot had almost cleared out, Nick couldn't help but be impressed by the different types of cars and trucks. He wondered if everyone in America owned an automobile, an idea that seemed ludicrous to him. He found himself fascinated with all the colors and shapes of the vehicles when Hank stopped in front of an older pick-up truck. A middle-aged woman emerged from a nearby car, and stood near the group.

Hank reached for her and slowly said the words, "Mabel, my wife."

Mabel smiled gently at the group of strangers. Her frame was petite. She wore a polka dot skirt that fell just below her knees and a cream sweater set. On her feet she wore pointed-toe black pumps. Her face bore an uncanny resemblance to that of Hank, weathered but framed with soft, wavy hair.

After an awkward moment, Hank gestured that it was time to get into the two vehicles.

"Well everyone," Nick said firmly, "let's get going." And with that instruction, the family quickly piled into the pick-up and car and headed toward the new life that waited for them.

Chapter Thirty-two

It was a short trip to the farm, and before they knew it, they turned onto a driveway and traveled down a long dirt road. They passed a large two-story home with a nearby garage. Nick assumed this was the main house. As they continued on, he saw the huge fields that waited for them. They finally pulled over and stopped. Doors opened quickly and everyone found themselves standing in front of a small wooden house with a tin roof and front porch. It wasn't large, but they would call it home for the next year. The front yard was unkempt, overrun with weeds, thistles, and tall grass.

Hank was first to walk toward the home, pointing toward it as if to say, "This is for you."

"I think this is for us," Nick told his family. He nodded back to Hank to show him he understood.

"Yes," Theresa replied, bringing her hands together, "This will do just fine."

"We'll get after those weeds in the morning," Eva said and she perused the yard. "After months of living in the barracks, this is a dream come true."

"We have a lot of work right here in the front yard to prepare for Christmas." Theresa said.

Mabel began walking toward the home inviting Theresa to follow her.

"She probably wants to show us around," Theresa said, walking toward her.

"Let's go in," Kati said. She and Leni began walking up the dirt path.

Theresa and Eva followed the girls up the path leading to the house.

Nicky was already unloading the suitcases out of the truck while Nick and his father remained behind wanting a moment with Hank. All three men were smiling. Nick could sense that this American had a good heart. He knew he had taken in many emigrants over the years and was experienced in the process. He had kind eyes, a warm handshake, and genuine smile that Nick was willing to wager he used often. If Nick could project how things would work out with Hank based on today, he had a pretty good inkling that things were going to move along just fine.

The months that followed passed so quickly, before Nick realized it, it was the end of February. Settling into their new home, re-establishing old routines, and becoming familiar with the farm's operations were top priorities. Every night after supper, Nick and Hank sat at the kitchen table with a new list of English words for Nick to learn. At first, the time spent with Hank was carefree and entertaining but lately, Nick could sense an element of urgency and assumed it had much to do with the looming task of tobacco planting.

There were other changes that had improved their lives too. With the help of the Jasinski family, another family of emigrants who lived across the street, Theresa and Leni had found work in a local shirt factory and Nicky as a butcher. The Jasinskis had a similar arrangement with Hank as Nick and his family -- after a year of service and minimum wage, they would fulfill their contract and be able to move on.

Nick and his father sat on the porch steps, shoulder-to-shoulder. The sun was setting and it was a spectacular array of purple, pink, orange and yellow. Nick was reflecting on a general feeling of disappointment that he had been carrying around all week.

"What is it, Nick? What's bothering you?" his father asked.

"I don't think Nicky wants to be a carpenter," he said, as he worked his toes into the sandy loam.

"He never liked carpentry, Nick, you know that." The older man puffed a few times on the pipe he held in his right hand, as he watched the sun's descent.

"I was hoping he would take to it after his internship in Salzburg."

"Hmm," his father replied.

"I had plans that we would open a shop of our own one day. Be our own boss and stop working for other people. But what does he do instead? A butcher! I'm so angry I could spit."

"He loves working with meat, Nick, just as you love working with wood. If you remember, I wanted you to become a tin maker, but you wouldn't have it."

"That was your dream for me, not mine."

"Aha!" his father said. "Does any of that sound familiar? He's 18. He's a man now. Let him choose his own way."

"That's hard to do."

"I know, but don't hold it against him, Nick. It

could cause a splinter so deep between you two it could change things forever. I know you don't want that to happen."

Nick exhaled, allowing his shoulders to slump. "I guess some dreams don't come true," he said.

Nick's father took in a deep breath and placed his hand lightly on Nick's back.

"Oh, Nick," he said softly, "that's life."

Chapter Thirty-three

In the months that followed, the gloom that had been plaguing Nick lifted. He felt better about Nicky after talking with his father and although it hurt and still bothered Nick at times, he wasn't going to let that come between him and his son. It was that simple. Besides, it wasn't as if Nick had time to ponder things. The spring had come and it was time to get the tobacco into the fields.

Since everyone else had jobs, Kati was left behind to help Nick plant. Nick's father took care of light repairs and replenishing the seedlings as needed. Luckily, Hank introduced Nick to a small planting machine that eased the burden. Nick was surprised to find that within a few weeks, they successfully finished the job. After getting cleaned up on their last night of planting, Hank shared with Nick some good news, and Nick couldn't wait to return home to tell his family.

Nick kept silent until the family was seated at the supper table. He placed a couple of pieces of fried chicken onto his plate and passed the platter to his father.

"Hank tells me that the Jasinski family has almost fulfilled their one-year contract," Nick said.

"Is that right?" his father asked. "When are they finished?"

"May."

"May?" Theresa asked. She passed the bowl of mashed potatoes to Leni, and then looked back at Nick.

"Nick, that's next month," she said. "I'm going to miss them."

"They've been good neighbors to us. If it weren't for them, Leni, Theresa, and Nicky wouldn't have found jobs as easily as they did. And, they drove you to work too!"

"What does their leaving mean to us?" Eva asked with a look of bewilderment. "I'll miss them too but that's how this program works. We stay a year and then we move on."

"Well, their house is bigger and Hank said it's ours if we want it." Nick beamed.

"Want it!" Theresa was the first to burst out her reply. "*Ja* we want it! Just think of what we can do with that extra room, Mother."

"Hank also tells me he has another family arriving by the name of Muellers from Mitrovica. They will move in here."

"Mitrovica?" Theresa asked, "My village?"

"*Ja*," Nick said, "I'm pretty sure Hank said their names are Henrick and Eva. I remembered that because she has the same first name as you, Mama."

Eva nodded and smiled back at Nick.

"Well," Theresa beamed, "I grew up with Eva. Her family was always good to me."

"And they have two children," Nick added, "Jacob and Rosi. They are as old as our Kati and Nicky."

"Hmmm," Eva's remark caught the attention of the other family members.

"What is it?" Nick asked.

"That could be trouble … teenagers living so close together. We'll have to watch them."

"*Ja, Oma!*" said Nicky. "You better watch us."

With that comment, the whole family burst out in hearty laughter and returned to their supper.

Chapter Thirty-four

When Memorial Day was a week away, the tobacco was swaying in the hot breeze. Nick found himself walking down the rows admiring the thick stalks that were beginning to show height. Flattening his hand, he felt the burly leaves, admiring their healthy color and texture.

After the Jasinkski family moved on, Nick was quick to move his family into the larger home. He felt happier than he had been in a long time. Maybe it was due to everyone working and a sense of really getting ahead, or maybe it was just that his family was finally safe from harm. An overwhelming feeling of excitement was felt by everyone but especially by Nick and Theresa, who finally believed their family was getting ahead.

Nick sat on the front porch steps as his father sat behind him in his favorite outdoor chair, enjoying his nightly pipe. Occasionally, they would share a few words, but overall they were simply enjoying the solace of the evening. With June nearing, the nights were warm, seldom cool enough to get a good night's sleep. Nick was amazed how fast the days flew by. Tending to the tobacco became an endless chore: the irrigation, weed control, and insect inspection were daily rituals. Nick thought about the day's work. He pictured Kati running barefoot through the tall rows, the sandy soil squeezing between her toes. Life had a predictable pattern and Nick felt most comfortable in routine.

Theresa waited on the other side of the screen door, allowing Nick and his father to finish their conversation. She and Eva had finished with the supper dishes. Leni and Kati had run off somewhere to enjoy the rest of the evening, and Nicky was sound asleep on the sofa.

"Hank asked me to drive in with him tomorrow to pick up the Mueller family," Nick had said to his father.

"Well, that would help since you speak their language. It was awfully confusing when we arrived. I remember that like yesterday."

"That's what Hank said. He also told me the Muellers will help us with the tobacco harvest, and we need the help."

"Theresa, Leni, and Nicky are still planning on quitting their jobs so they can help too, right?"

"They are," Nick answered, "but we're going to need more help than that. Once the leaves start turning yellow, they need to be picked, hauled to the barn to dry, and stored until we go to market."

"Well, it's good thing the Muellers are arriving now, before the harvest. Eight more hands will make a big difference," his father added.

Theresa opened the screen door and stepped out onto the porch joining the two men.

Nick immediately shuffled over on the steps to make room for her. "I was just telling Father that the Muellers are coming tomorrow," he told her.

"I'm excited to see them," Theresa said as she sat down next to her husband. "It will be good to be around our own people again. I miss the Jasinkskis more than I thought I would."

Nick had to admit that he was excited as well, but not for the social reasons Theresa mentioned. He needed the manual labor and would welcome the Muellers with open arms.

Later that evening, Nick could feel the aches and pains from a long day's work. His body was tired. Despite his exhaustion, he simply had too much on his mind to fall asleep. He turned toward Theresa hoping she had not yet drifted off and was glad to see her looking back at him.

"You know, Theresa," Nick whispered, "the debt for our passage is now paid. Last week, I was able to put money into our savings."

"Oh, Nick, already? Theresa said a bit surprised.

"*Ja,*" Nick continued to speak in hushed tones. "We are now building a nest egg toward our future."

"I forgot to tell you about the letter I received from Maria."

"Your half-sister?"

"*Ja.* She tells me that we should move to Milwaukee once our contract is up. She said there are people from Calma settling there!"

"From Calma?" Nick asked. "Did she say who?"

"The Beckers from across the village and the Engel family."

"Engel?" Nick couldn't remember them.

"You remember Hans Engel. He sold us the ducks."

"Ah," Nick said.

"Nick, wouldn't it be wonderful to live near our

own people again? North Carolina is not for us. After all, the girls are deathly afraid of the snakes that seem to be everywhere here. And you, Nick – you have trouble with this stifling heat."

"Ugh," Nick moaned.

"Admit it!" Theresa demanded.

Nick knew that Theresa was pressing for the move. The thought of living near her half-sister, Maria, was no doubt attractive to her.

"Theresa, you do remember that we have another six or seven months left on our contract with Hank before we can go anywhere. We have the tobacco harvest first, then the sweet potatoes."

"I know," she said, "but we can think about Milwaukee, right?"

"Right," Nick agreed. "I think it's worth thinking about."

"I do too," Theresa said quickly. "After all, we have family there."

Nick rolled over onto his side, forcing his eyes closed. Theresa was right; it would be nice to be around people from Calma. The more Nick thought about it, the more sense it made.

But, for the time being, he was a farmer, and a farmer's schedule had little time to squander. Sweet potato planting was now upon them and this time, he and Kati were on their own. Hank would not be there to help them along. Nick rolled onto his back and placed both of his hands behind his head trying to envision the next day's labor. He would use the same planting machine for the sweet potatoes that he used for the tobacco. Although Nick had some experience with the machine, he questioned his own expertise. What if the machine jammed? Or they didn't make good time? He wondered just how simple a task this was going to be without Hank and with a stubborn old donkey to guide the planter.

He stared into the blackness listening to the soft sounds his wife made in her slumber. Turning toward her, he edged nearer and felt the night's breeze wafting in from a nearby window. Nick's lids suddenly felt heavy. He pulled the light comforter up to his chin, and letting his body relax, he drifted off to sleep.

Chapter Thirty-five

The next morning, Theresa and Leni were in the kitchen preparing their lunches for work. Nick was enjoying his coffee, thinking about the task that lay ahead of him. He was about to take the first bite of his buttered toast, when he noticed that Kati had pulled Leni away and was talking to her softly. Straining to overhear their conversation, Nick almost toppled off his chair. Eva, who was seated across the table from him, snickered.

Nick winked back at his mother but quickly turned his attention back to his girls.

"Why don't you stay and help *Datee* with the sweet potatoes," Kati said under her breath, hoping her father would not hear, "and I will go to work at that shirt factory."

"Kati!" Leni shrieked. "You can't work yet – you are not old enough, and I am too old to stay home. *Datee* said I have to work until the tobacco harvest."

"Ssshh!" Kati scolded while looking over her shoulder. "I had to help *Datee* with the tobacco planting."

"*Ja!* That's your job, remember?" Leni whispered.

"It is not my job!" Kati fumed. "The farmer is not paying me for my work. He is only paying *Datee.*"

"What are you two jabbering about?" Nick asked. He now stood behind the two girls.

"Nothing, *Datee,*" Kati replied.

"Very well, Katarina, let's get going. We have a full day's work ahead of us."

Turning away from Leni, Kati walked past her grandmother, who was still seated at the kitchen table. The kitchen door banged twice with her exit.

Smiling first at Leni, Nick turned on his heels and walked toward Theresa. Laying his hand on the top of her back, he kissed her lips then followed his youngest daughter outside. Bounding down the porch steps, Nick stopped for a moment to look at a thick haze suspended over the field as far as his eyes could see. It would be another hot one, Nick was certain. Slapping at a mosquito that had landed on the back of his neck, he quickened his gait, and caught up to Kati. They walked side-by-side, then Nick placed his hand on her shoulder, and the two made their way to the barn.

Nick had a plan for today and it was a simple one. He figured if he kept things less complicated, the fewer problems he would run into. Kati would help keep the machine stocked with sweet potatoes, and he would steer the donkey down the rows. Nick had his doubts that the day would run smoothly, but it was a job that had to get done, and he and Kati were going to do it. Between the donkey and Kati's ability to keep pace with the planter, he suspected he was in for a morning of aggravation.

Nick never welcomed the sound of his mother's voice calling him for lunch, more than he did today. As he expected, minor irritations grew to major frustrations. He lost his temper too many times to count and every time he raised his voice, the donkey stopped dead in his tracks, assuming Nick was commanding him to do so, while Kati cowered. The situation got the best of Nick several times, and he found himself swearing to the heavens for patience, mercy, and a way out of this miserable job. He was a carpenter, not a farmer! How did he ever end up in the middle of a hot, dusty field in North Carolina? *"Lord, have mercy!"* he cried out loud.

Nick now stood at the end of a planted row, with a smile on his face. The day was over, the sun now setting. He never imagined that things would end up running smoothly, but they did. Kati seemed to have a better grasp on what she had to do and the donkey trudged along seemingly ignoring Nick's occasional outbursts. The days that followed held the same pattern and by the week's end, the job that had seemed so daunting was finished.

Nick and Kati stood proudly before the field, admiring the straight rows, now laden with sweet potatoes beneath the dirt. The planting season had officially ended!

"You did good, Katarina," Nick said.

"Really, *Datee?*" she asked.

Nick turned toward Kati wondering if he had been too hard on her. He knew he wasn't a patient man, oftentimes the opposite, especially when it involved the children. That was Theresa's job, and he had to admit, he relied upon her to keep the peace. But Theresa wasn't here, and he suddenly realized it was up to him to make this right.

"Really," he said to Kati. Looking into her eyes, he rested both of his hands on her shoulders. "I'm proud of what we did here. I couldn't have done it without you."

Kati smiled broadly back at her father and Nick knew his words had touched her.

They eventually turned away from the field and headed home. Nick thought about how they had entered the field, as two common laborers, but they were leaving as father and daughter once again. He placed his hand on Kati's shoulder. And as the job had begun, they walked from the barn back to the house connected.

Nick's spirits were immediately lifted when he and Kati entered the house and heard Eva's humming. He watched as she labored over the stove. An aroma of pungent paprika filled the room. She delicately placed the large pot in the center of the table and lifted the cover. Nick could see the bubbling rich gravy surrounding large pieces of chicken, thick slices of onions, and cloves of garlic. Billows of steam rose to the ceiling.

"*Oma*! That smells delicious," Kati said.

"Chicken *paprikash*," she announced. Her cheeks were reddened and her hair matted down at the crown, but she, like Nick and Kati, stood proud over a job well done. A loaf of homemade bread rested on a cutting board, a slab of butter close by. Cream-colored dumplings sprinkled with sautéed breadcrumbs and freshly cut green beans tossed with crisp bacon decorated the table. And as if Eva had rung a dinner bell, the family gathered around the table and the frustrations of the day were no more.

Chapter Thirty-six

With the planting season behind him, all Nick had to do now was wait. Wait for the tobacco to season, for the sweet potatoes to flower, and for the rain and the heat to make it all happen. And it did. By July, the tobacco leaves swayed in the wind and the sweet potatoes showcased pretty white flowers with purple centers. Nick's stood with pride as he surveyed the crops. Yet, when he was honest with himself, he knew he longed to return to the life of a cabinet maker.

Spending time with Hank these past several weeks talking about the steps he would need to take for the harvest helped Nick feel ready to direct his family in the roles they would play. But first, he wanted to talk with Theresa. He walked around to the backyard and found her in the garden pulling weeds with his mother.

"Nick!" she said with a hint of surprise in her voice. Nick typically spent Saturday afternoons with Hank at a nearby fishing hole. It had become a Saturday afternoon tradition followed by a big pot of fish goulash for supper.

"I want to talk something over with you, Theresa," Nick said.

"Oh?" Theresa asked. "What is it?"

"Milwaukee."

"Maria sent me another letter about that," Theresa added.

Eva stiffened. She had witnessed more than one conversation about Milwaukee. She didn't care to get caught in the middle between her son and her daughter-in-law. She loved them both too much and understood her boundaries.

Nick could hear the excitement in Theresa's voice. He softened. She had been urging him to commit to the move for a couple of months now. As the letters from Maria continued, the urgency in Theresa's voice grew stronger.

"Maria said more families from Calma are moving to Milwaukee. Nick, they have dances on Saturday nights and German movies on Sunday afternoons!" Theresa drove her hoe into the rich garden dirt, giving weight to her argument while Eva stood quietly nearby, watching and listening to the exchange.

"Well, Theresa," Nick said. The corners of his right eye crinkled in a wink in his mother's direction. "When we finish the tobacco, how would you feel about sending Leni on the train to Maria's? She can look for an apartment for us, and we can begin to make plans to move to Milwaukee."

"Oh, Nick!" Letting the hoe fall to the ground, Theresa ran awkwardly down the garden row, practically falling into Nick's arms.

"*Datee,* I would love to go!" Leni popped up from her hiding place behind a high row of green pole beans.

"Leni!" Nick said with a look of surprise. "I'm sure you would!"

Chapter Thirty-seven

After supper, Nick looked around at his family gathered on the front porch. "Well, Hank has explained to me how he wants the tobacco harvested," Nick began. "Leni and Theresa, it's time you put your notice in at the shirt factory. You'll both be needed here."

Leni and Theresa shared a passing glance and nodded to one another.

"What do we do first?" Nicky asked.

"Well, we start by plucking the yellow leaves off the bottom of the plants. It means a lot of picking, but we'll have help. Since the pickles are done, the Muellers will come over every morning to help us. Workers will also be trucked in."

Nick could see the look that crossed Kati's face. He sensed that she and the Mueller boy were sweet on each other. Jacob had been coming over quite a bit lately. He had even offered to help with cooking supper. Nick suspected Jacob's intentions were to get closer to his youngest daughter. At the same time, Nicky was giving an awful lot of attention to Rosi, Jacob's younger sister. But what bothered Nick even more was Hank's suggestion that Leni consider marrying his nephew. According to Hank, his nephew had been looking for a wife for more than 10 years! The more Nick thought about it, the more nerves it struck. He didn't want Leni to experience what Theresa did so many years ago, the misery of an arranged marriage. Nick did not want Leni staying behind in North Carolina. No! No! No! That was one of the reasons why he suggested she make the trip to Milwaukee.

"There are some yellow ones out there already, *Datee,*" Kati said, bringing Nick back to the conversation.

Nick nodded his head in agreement. "Those are the ones we want to take off the plant, but we want to leave the green ones."

"Do we haul the yellow ones up to the barn?" Nicky asked.

"*Ja,* I'll use the wagon and take them up to barn where Leni and Theresa will tie them onto the tobacco sticks so they can dry. They call that curing. They'll hang in the barn for a couple of months."

"Tell them the good news, Nick," Theresa interrupted, her face beaming.

Nick took in a deep breath and addressed the group. "When we are all done with the tobacco, Leni will take the train to your Aunt Maria's."

"Are we moving to Wisconsin?" Nicky asked with a hopeful look. "Because that's where I want to go!"

"Really?" Nick asked, turning toward his son. Nick had been unaware he had an opinion on the move.

"Mother said they have dances on Saturday nights!" Nicky said.

"You know the Muellers are thinking about moving there too," Kati added.

"Oh?" Nick asked. "And how is it that you know

this, Katarina?"

"Jacob told me."

"Ah, Jacob, again!" Nick said, but followed his gruff response with a soft smile toward his youngest daughter.

Chapter Thirty-eight

When fall arrived, the time came to truck the tobacco to auction. Now dried, crinkled, and discolored, it lay in bundles in the back of the truck and trailer. Nick rode along with Hank, as he did on most errands. The two men had become almost inseparable.

The auction house was not what Nick had expected. A large warehouse welcomed buyers and sellers through expansive, open doors. The musty smell of tobacco filled Nick's nostrils, and he had to admit, it didn't bother him one bit. As a smoker himself, he rather enjoyed the aroma.

After getting the tobacco unloaded, Nick watched the buyers walk up and down the aisles examining the leaves. Unsure of what they were looking for, Nick continued to watch them until the auctioneer bellowed to start the bidding and the "dance" began.

"One dollar bid, now two, now two," the auctioneer sang out.

Nick's head was spinning. He struggled to keep up with the sing-song words that spilled from the auctioneer's mouth. The whole process moved so quickly and before Nick knew it, Hank's tobacco was sold, and it was all over.

"Well, what did you think, Nick?"

"I never knew someone could talk so fast!"

"I told you, a tobacco auction is the greatest show on Earth!" Hank said while slapping Nick's back.

As they made their way to the truck, Nick wished he could experience it all over again, but he knew that he never would, not now, with the move to Milwaukee looming.

The ride home from the auction was quiet. Nick stretched his feet out in front of him, biding his time. He wanted to broach the subject of cutting his contract short and moving when Hank's spirits were high. Nick figured Hank's good mood was a direct result of the profit he made on his tobacco. This was as a good a time as any.

"You know, Hank, we're thinking on moving up to Wisconsin," Nick blurted. His stomach lurched, his mouth feeling as dry as North Carolina dirt.

"Wisconsin! Nick, do you know how cold it is up there? You don't want to do that."

"Well," Nick said, feeling his throat tighten. He did not want this conversation to take a bad turn.

"Theresa has a half-sister, Maria, who lives up there."

"Is that right?" Hank asked.

"*Ja!*" Nick said feeling a little more at ease. "She's been telling Theresa that people from our village are moving there."

"From Calma? Aw, Nick, I'd hate to see you go. You're different from the rest."

Nick looked over at Hank realizing that they had become buddies. He would genuinely miss Hank.

As the miles slipped away, the two men came to an agreement. Nick would be temporarily released from his contract with the promise to return for the sweet potato harvest. Hank would need his help with that but he agreed to officially sign off on the contract as soon as the job was done. Just after twilight, they pulled into the farm, two happy men but for two very different reasons.

After saying goodnight to Hank, Nick quickened his steps to the house. He wanted to sit down with Leni to make sure she was ready for the trip to Milwaukee tomorrow.

As he entered the room, Nick heard Theresa say to Leni, "There is a young lady living with Aunt Maria right now about your age, Leni. Make sure you make friends with her and let her show you around." Both women were seated at the kitchen table.

"Nick," Theresa said while turning toward him. "How did it go at the auction?"

"It went well for Hank. I think he got a good price for the crop."

"Did you tell Hank about Milwaukee? What about the contract? Can we leave early?"

Nick waved his hand back and forth and grimaced, signaling to Theresa "not now." Leni's trip north was clouding his mind, his concerns for her were mounting.

"*Datee,* may I go with Leni to Milwaukee tomorrow?" Kati asked as she shot up from her chair in the living room. Her blue eyes peered into his and Nick could sense her excitement.

Nick walked toward her. He had been half-expecting this question from her and laying his hands on her shoulders, he spoke with tenderness.

"Kati, I need you here to help your mother.

There's packing and cleaning and your grandparents need your help here. It won't be long and your sister will find us a place to live. I'm sure of that." Nick looked over at Leni and noticed an immediate smile.

"Ooookay," Kati droned. Her shoulders slumped as she shuffled her feet back to her chair and plopped down.

Nick hated to disappoint her, but had no choice. He turned and walked toward the table, pulled out a chair, and sat down.

"Now, Leni," he began, "I want you to look around and be aware tomorrow. Don't depend on strangers to help you. And whatever you do, don't talk to anyone! You will be traveling with money, so you need to be careful."

*"Datee!"*Leni shrieked. "I'm 20 years old. I know what to do!"

Nick stretched his arms toward her and grasped her hands within his. "I know you know, Magdalena. But I just need to tell you anyway."

A soft smile replaced the angry voice, as Leni looked into the eyes of her father.

Chapter Thirty-nine

The trip north to Milwaukee was uneventful for Leni. True to her father's words, she found the perfect rental for them on 4th Street. With her Aunt Maria's help, they located a small but nice two bedroom home just a few blocks away from her aunt's. Nick read her letter out loud the day it arrived in the mail.

August 18, 1952

To My Family,

I have found the most beautiful little house for us. It is located on 4th Street in Milwaukee. It has two big bedrooms, a yellow kitchen, and a big living room. It even has a nice backyard so *Oma* can have her garden. And, it is completely furnished! It is only a few blocks away from Aunt Maria's house. Isn't this wonderful!

I have paid the security deposit and the first month's rent from the money you have sent along with me. And, yes, *Datee,* I was very careful to count it out properly and receive a receipt.

I know you will love Milwaukee as

much as I do already. It is nothing like North Carolina. It feels like home. The weather is warm and some people say, 'fall is in the air.' I'm not sure what that means, but it is pretty here.

There is much to do here too. On Saturday nights, we go to Jefferson Hall and dance and sing. They have German bands playing for us. And on Sundays, we can walk to the theatre to see a movie in German!

But, I have saved the best for last. I have seen the Becker and Faust families from Calma! Isn't that good news! Please come soon, your new home is waiting.

All my love,
Leni

After reading the letter out loud, Nick folded it in thirds and slipped it into his shirt pocket. His face could not hide the pride he was feeling for his daughter. She had done it. He looked into the eyes of his wife, who had been watching him during the entire reading.

"Well, it looks like our Leni did a fine job," he said.

"It sounds wonderful, absolutely perfect!" Theresa agreed, bringing her hands together, "and only a few blocks from Maria's house. When can we leave, Nick?"

Nick's father leaned forward in his chair. "What about the sweet potatoes?" he asked.

"I'm planning on coming back. I gave Hank my

word." Nick looked over the heads of his family, toward his father.

"What about the Muellers?" Kati asked. "Will they be coming with us to Wisconsin?"

"Katarina Russ!" Nick blurted, while turning on his heels to face Kati. "Why have you so concerned yourself with the Muellers?"

Kati's cheeks flared a crimson red, her eyes drifting to the floor boards.

"Well, are they?" she whispered.

"Yes, sweetheart," Theresa intervened, stepping toward her daughter. "As a matter of fact, Jacob's mother told me yesterday that they will be moving north with us." She placed both of her hands onto Kati's shoulders and smiled.

Kati breathed a sigh of relief, returned the smile to her mother, and took a seat next to her brother, Nicky, on the sofa.

Turning toward Nick, Theresa suggested a seat near the children. She placed her right hand on top of his. Nick felt the calm that came over him with her touch, inwardly questioning his own reaction to Kati's simple question.

"The Muellers arrived here a few short months ago," Nick Sr. said. He puffed his pipe to reignite the burn. When satisfied, he leaned forward. "How can they leave so soon?"

"They came in May," Nick said nodding as he spoke. "But Hank said he'd release them early."

"Early?" Eva asked. She rested the afghan she was crocheting on her lap as she looked up at Nick.

"Apparently, he has nothing for them to do,"

Nick explained, shrugging his shoulders.

"Isn't that nice?" Eva said, with a smile.

"Is it?" Nick asked.

Why did Nick feel that he was missing something? What did it matter if the Muellers left at the same time? He wasn't sure but made a mental note to discuss it with Theresa later. Certainly, she would explain it to him.

Nick turned his attention back to Kati. He noticed the contented look that came over her face and heard the sigh when Theresa told her the Muellers were coming with them to Milwaukee. Unnoticed, he continued to watch her, as she and Nicky spoke softly to one another. Nick could only wonder what that was all about.

Chapter Forty

On a warm autumn morning in 1952, the Russ and Mueller families loaded their luggage onto the train destined for Milwaukee. Nick could almost touch the excitement in the air. He and Theresa took their seats directly behind his parents and the Muellers chose seats across the aisle. Kati and Nicky headed for the back with Jacob and Rosi on their heels.

As the wheels of the locomotive turned, Nick felt content. Theresa seemed almost giddy with the move now underway. He slipped his arm around her shoulders. She looked up at him and smiled, resting her head on his chest. He said nothing to her because he knew it was one of those moments where words were unnecessary. Instead, he snuggled in against her, closed his eyes, and fell into a peaceful sleep.

Hours passed with multiple stops to allow more passengers to board the train. Nick drifted in and out of sleep throughout the day. Shadows danced across his closed eyelids. Squinting at first, he opened his eyes wide to find the Midwest alive with color. It appeared as a collage of huge billowy trees that splashed reds, golds, browns and oranges as the train stayed its course.

As the family traveled through Wisconsin, the panoramic array of colors that spilled out in front of them practically took their breath away. They rode in silence with the exception of an occasional ohh or ahh. Theresa nudged Nick to get his attention. She motioned with her head toward Kati who was standing, trying her best to force a small window open. Jacob's strong hands were upon hers in a moment. In a flash, the window easily slid free of its rusted prison. Nick brought his finger to his lip, resting his chin on his thumb, and pondered a moment. Had he noticed Jacob trading seats in order to sit with Kati? He couldn't remember. Watching them, Nick noticed her lingering gaze on Jacob, the smile that etched across her face. Soon, other windows were being pried open in the same manner, distracting Nick from his observations. The dry scent of burning leaves slowly filled the train car.

"Certainly, we've enjoyed beautiful autumns in Calma, but nothing compared to this," Nick Sr. said.

"If this is what fall is like, I wonder what else Wisconsin has to offer us?" Eva asked.

"Whatever it is," Nick said as he turned back around in his seat, "we can handle it."

The train arrived at the Milwaukee train depot just before supper. Maria was waiting for them. A broad smile decorated her face.

"Leni is waiting for you at your house," she said to the group when they were finally all together.

"Oh! How wonderful. We'll get to see it tonight?" Theresa asked.

"Oh, yes, yes, of course. She's so excited for you to see it."

"Do you have room for all of us?" Nick asked. He scanned the nearby parking lot as if to recognize the automobile Maria had arranged for them.

"Of course, follow me," she said.

Picking up their luggage, the family followed behind Maria, who led the pack while chatting with Theresa.

Leni stood on the front porch of the rental she had found for her family. She was holding a large picnic basket that she swung from side to side, in order to pass the time. When she spotted her Aunt Maria's car heading down the street, a toothy smile emerged. Looking at her now, Nick realized just how much he had missed her.

"Welcome home," Leni cried out when her family got out of the vehicle. Setting the basket down on the porch, she ran toward her family.

"Hello, Leni," Theresa was the first to greet her, stretching her arms out wide.

"Well, my little *schatzi*," Nick said. Although Leni was twenty years old, Nick still enjoyed using the childhood nickname he chose for all of his children. "Let's take a look at this house you found for us."

Leni bowed, waving her arm as if presenting the house to her father, then bolted ahead taking the porch steps two-by-two. Picking up the picnic basket with her right hand, she opened the screen door, and began the tour. Leni pointed out all the special features she could remember from her meeting with the landlord: a small amount of steps that her *Ota* would have to climb at both the front and back entrances; the spacious living room that would easily accommodate sleeping quarters for her brother; a soft yellow kitchen facing east allowing morning sunlight; the garage where her father might find room for a small workbench; and finally, saving the best feature for last, a bedroom for her parents of their very own. It had been such a very long time since they had that simple luxury.

When the tour ended, the family gathered in the kitchen; Theresa and Eva paying more attention now to their workspace. Leni set the basket on top of the kitchen table and began unwrapping and arranging thinly sliced cuts of German bologna, shinkenwurst, yahtwurst and assorted cheeses she had purchased from the German deli earlier that day. She hoped she had thought of everything.

"Oh, Leni," her mother said, as she moved toward her. Her hands fell to her chest, eyes moist.

"You did a fine job, Leni," her father told her, hands resting on his hips, "a fine job. Now, the next thing we must do is find work." He walked over to the chair at the head of the table and seated himself. His family followed his lead.

"Well, actually," Leni said, "I'd like to introduce you to someone who might be able to help us with that."

"Oh? Who is that?" Nick asked as he laid a piece of Limburger cheese onto his roll.

Leni motioned toward a young man standing in the doorway. A bit surprised he hadn't heard the stranger enter the house, Nick's eyes narrowed. A tall, handsome young man stood in the doorway.

"Hello, Mr. Russ," the stranger said. He walked toward Nick with an extended hand. "I'm Nikolaus Schimpf."

Nick stood and grabbed hold of the strong hand before him. He immediately noticed a broad smile, a head full of light hair, and striking blue eyes. His .build was lean and he appeared taller than Nick, just under six foot. But it was his contagious smile that was most appealing. In an instant, Nikolaus stood next to Leni, and Nick began piecing it all together.

"I left Germany with my parents in '51," he explained. "We came over on the General Moore. Hello, Mrs. Russ," he said to Theresa, then nodded at Nick's parents and his son, Nicky.

"And you must be Kati." Nikolaus leaned toward her with special attention. "Leni has told me so much about you." Kati returned the attention with flushed cheeks, lips curling in a soft smile.

"Join us for lunch?" Theresa asked. She motioned to a vacant chair at the table.

"*Dankeschön*," Nikolaus said and quickly took a seat next to Leni.

"When in '51?" Nick's father asked, curious about the stranger.

"September 15." Nikolaus said. "We live here in Milwaukee now on 24th and Galena."

"I see," Nick said, turning his head toward Leni.

Leni met her father's questioning gaze. She shrugged her shoulders and smiled, her cheeks blushing from a quiet pink to a soft red.

"How is it that you know our Leni?"

"We met at a wedding. As soon as I laid eyes on her, I knew."

"Knew?" Nick asked. "Knew what?"

"You remember, *Datee*," Leni interrupted, "the wedding Aunt Maria and Uncle Joe took me to."

"Hmmm," Nick replied turning from Leni back to Nikolaus.

"What did you say your parents' names are?"

"He didn't say," Theresa said, "give the young man a chance, Nick."

"Maria and Michael Schimpf," Nikolaus said without hesitation.

"Are they working?" Nick persisted with his litany.

"*Ja*," Nikolaus replied. "My stepfather works at the Milwaukee Athletic Club as a butcher. My mother is a housekeeper."

In what appeared to be an effortless, practiced manner, Leni's hand had found her young man's. Suddenly, Nick felt as if he were on the outside looking in and knew he had asked enough questions for a day.

"How soon before you're ready to go to work, Mr. Russ? I may have a few job leads you may find interesting." Nikolaus offered.

"That's awfully kind of you," Nick said, holding a smile.

Chapter Forty-one

Theresa looked over at Leni and smiled. She placed a head of lettuce in the grocery cart and paused a moment watching her daughter pick through a mound of pears. Time alone with Leni had become so infrequent that Theresa actually missed moments like these, the simple tasks that drew a mother and daughter together.

Most of Leni's free time was now spent with Nikolaus. In fact, she was seldom home at all anymore, often preferring to go dancing or meeting up with their friends. Her life was moving forward in an exciting direction that did not include her parents. Theresa told Nick it was natural, and they both could see that their daughter had fallen in love with Nikolaus, and things would soon change in their family.

"Leni, do you enjoy working at the glove factory?" Theresa asked. The two women had been employed at Midwest Leathers for nearly three months now.

"*Ja*, it's okay," Leni said. "Nikolaus said he can help me find a new job if I want to, but I'm not sure. . ."

"Not sure, Leni?"

"I know you're happy there, and I don't want to leave you behind."

"Oh, Leni," Theresa smiled. "Your life is going to

take you to places I can't go. You know that."

"I know," Leni said with some reluctance. She began pushing the half-filled cart for her mother. "I'm just not ready to make the move right now."

"Okay," Theresa said, but stopped walking and faced her daughter. "We can always talk, you and I, no matter where life takes you."

"Are you talking about Nikolaus? Because he said he would never take me far from my family."

Theresa nodded but suddenly realized that Leni and Nikolaus had actually discussed having a future together. This was getting serious!

"All I'm saying, Leni, is that your father and I will be okay, and you should live the life you are meant to live."

"Okay. But I have a feeling we won't be far from each other. I hope I'm right."

"Me too," Theresa said. She began walking down the store aisle, Leni following with the cart behind her.

"What did you work on today?" Nick asked Theresa while lending a hand with the grocery bags.

"Football skins," she said.

"Hmm," Nick said. He was grateful his family had found jobs, and he had Nikolaus to thank for it. He had come through for them, just as he said he would.

Leni followed Nick, carrying the last bag.

"Is Kati home yet?" Leni asked. Kati worked part-time hours at a local laundromat while finishing her last year in high school.

"*Ja*, she's upstairs," Nick said and watched Leni exit the kitchen.

"What about Nicky, is he home too?" Theresa asked.

"No. And why he wants to work in a slaughterhouse is beyond me."

Theresa could sense that the same old argument brewing behind Nick's eyes and regretted asking him about their son.

"He tried working as a carpenter's apprentice: once in Salzburg and again here in Milwaukee. And he did it for you, Nick, because you wanted him to try it!"

Nick sat down at the kitchen table and sighed. His shoulders slumped forward as he laced his fingers together.

Theresa moved toward him. Laying her nimble fingers on his shoulders, she began kneading.

"You have to let it go, Nick," she said. "He's happy as a butcher. Be happy for him."

"I know," Nick replied weakly. Nick's dream for his son to follow in his footsteps was slowly fading from sight. He knew Theresa was right but what he couldn't figure out was how to stop the anger that festered inside of him every time he thought about his son following a different path than his own.

"You know," Theresa said bringing him out of his own thoughts, "Nicky is spending just as much time with Rosi as Leni is spending with Nikolaus."

"*Ja*," Nick said, relieved the subject had changed. "And what about Kati and Jacob? They are also together too much."

"Too much?

"Kati is only 17."

"What do you mean, Nick? This is life. Our

children move on and build their own lives. Leni is 20 years old. And Nick is 18!"

"And us? What is to become of us?" Nick asked.

Theresa smiled, looking at him. He appeared almost childlike to her, face flushed, eyes dampened at the edges. Nudging his arms open, she placed her small frame in his lap.

"We start where we began, Nick," she said while stroking the side of his face with her palm. "Remember?" she asked, a smile stretching across her face.

Their eyes met and lips touched.

"I remember," Nick said. He pulled back to look at her. Nick slowly helped her to her feet, enclosed her hand in his, and led her to their room, gently closing the door behind them.

Nick raised his champagne glass and gently clinked it against his wife's. "To one of the best years of our lives," he said. Tipping their glasses to their lips, the cold bubbly spirits slid down easily, the effervescence nipping at their noses.

"This past year was everything we hoped it would be," Theresa said, and then took another small swallow from her glass.

"Remember when we all lived in one room in Austria and in Salzburg?" Nick asked. He knew Theresa would never forget their past. He looked at her now, hoping the life she had with him was the one she had envisioned.

"I'm glad North Carolina is behind us," Theresa said.

She hadn't liked it when Nick returned to help Hank with the sweet potato harvest, but Nick had refused to budge on the subject. He kept true to his agreement and made the trip back. He was paid handsomely but was secretly relieved to get back on the train to Milwaukee to his family and his job as a cabinet maker.

"And now, we are about to buy our first home!" Nick said. He shook his head from side to side. "I never would have thought..."

"Maria was right about Milwaukee," Theresa said. "It was the best decision we ever made."

It was true. With everyone in the family working good jobs, a steady income flowed into the household. Saving money toward a down payment for a home was easy.

Chapter Forty-two

As the January winds blew, Nick felt that the days and weeks turned over with an incredible slowness. He disliked the bitter winds of Wisconsin's winter and couldn't understand how people could bear it. He quickened his steps making his way home. It was Friday, and he had pushed himself all week at work in order to finish his latest project. Although he was in his early forties, there were days he felt much older. Today was one of those days.

When Nick opened the back door and entered the kitchen, he found Leni and Nikolaus seated at the table. He instantly felt a surge of warm air meet his face. He closed the door firmly behind him, unbuttoned his coat, and removed his hat, hanging them on the pegs near the door. Working his galoshes off, he let them fall onto the floor with a wet, heavy thud.

"Hello, Mr. Russ," Nikolaus said, a smile stretched from ear to ear. Leni sat beside him.

"Nikolaus, Leni," Nick nodded in the couple's direction while rubbing both hands together. Nick had grown used to seeing Nikolaus in his home. He and Leni spent almost every Friday and Saturday night together and oftentimes, Nikolaus would be a guest for Sunday soup after Mass. On occasion, he would stop by for a few hours during the work week as well.

Keeping to his nightly ritual, Nick carried his lunchbox over to the counter, toward Theresa. She was facing the sink, scrubbing the skins of red potatoes. His mother was stirring a pot of homemade sausage and peppers bubbling on the stove. The pungent steam billowed and caused Nick's mouth to water. After giving his mother a quick wink, he spoke under his breath to Theresa.

"Hello, darling," he said. "Dinner smells delicious." Nick said while placing his lunchbox on the counter next to the sink.

"How was it today?" Theresa asked, her eyes remaining on her task.

"I finished varnishing the table." He rested both of his hands on his hips.

"Your father's lying down," Eva interrupted. "Could you wake him for supper?"

"*Ja*, I'll go wash up." As he left the room, he could feel Nikolaus and Leni's eyes follow him but wondered why?

Later that evening, Nick sighed as he sat down in his favorite chair in the living room, newspaper in hand. Theresa was busy crocheting, counting under her breath: "forty-four, forty-five." The cream-colored afghan lay across her lap, cascading across her knees. It would probably be just the two of them tonight. Nick's parents had already turned in, and Nicky and Kati were on a double date with Rosi and Jacob. Although Nikolaus and Leni were finishing up the supper dishes, Nick suspected they would say their goodnights, heading out to a movie or meeting up with their friends.

"Tired?" Theresa asked, still focused on her stitches. She heard Nick's moan as he positioned himself in his chair.

"*Ja,*" Nick said, "Some days are easier than others. Even though I finished the table ..." Nick was interrupted by the sudden movement of Theresa's head. He followed her gaze to Leni entering the room, Nikolaus was right behind her.

"*Datee?* Could we speak with you?" Leni asked. Nikolaus stepped forward in order to stand side-by-side with Leni. Silently and without notice, Theresa placed the afghan on her lap. Between the fingers of her right hand, she repeatedly rolled the crochet hook forward and then backwards, a habit Nick had grown used to.

"Of course," Nick placed the newspaper down onto the cocktail table in front of him and leaned forward, placing his forearms on his thighs. He nodded toward the loveseat across the room for the couple to sit down.

"Mr. Russ, I hope you know how much Leni means to me," Nikolaus began. His arms dropped to his sides. As if timed perfectly, Leni opened her left hand, wrapping her fingers around his.

"I mean," Nikolaus struggled, "since the moment I saw her at the wedding last summer, I just knew." His eyes drifted to Leni's. They exchanged one of the warm looks Nick had grown accustomed to seeing between them.

"I just can't imagine life without her," Nikolaus said. He finger-combed back his hair.

Theresa placed her hand on Nick's leg, a cue for Nick to relax, to listen. Nick drew in a deep breath and inched back in his chair, trying to ease the young man's painful discomfort.

"So, what I'm saying," Nikolaus said, then paused. "I mean, what I'm asking, Mr. Russ, is for your blessing to marry your daughter."

Nick heard Theresa softly gasp as she brought her fingertips to her lips.

Time stood still. In the silence, Nick noticed the quiet ticking of the clock on the adjacent wall, the rhythmic moans of the coal furnace running in the basement. Clearing his throat, he turned his head toward Theresa. Their eyes met. His mind raced and heart followed.

At once, a catalog of questions plagued him. *How do I recognize a good man? An honest man? Nikolaus has a good job at Allis Chalmers. He is diligent with his money. He isn't a selfish man but probably one of the most generous I have ever met. Hadn't he bought Leni a gold watch with diamonds this past Christmas?* More importantly, Nick knew the young man loved her deeply. And she, him. *Isn't that what I always wanted for my little girl?*

"Datee?" Leni's voice jolted Nick back to the present.

Nick snapped his head toward the couple who waited for his response, startled by the interruption from his own thoughts.

"Well," Nick said, a smirk appearing across his face. Theresa recognized the look and knew to expect the unexpected from her husband. "You know she's not very healthy," he said to Nikolaus, "but if you want her, you can have her!"

Nikolaus threw back his head in hearty laughter. He extended his hand to Nick, "I'm not too worried," he said with confidence.

While the two men shook hands, Theresa stood up from her chair, afghan dropping onto the floor, crochet hook rolling toward the wall.

"Leni, Leni," she repeated with excitement, her hands coming together.

Leni scurried over to her mother with open arms, and the two women embraced.

"Well, how does May 30th sound to everyone?" Nikolaus asked.

"Theresa?" Nick looked to his wife for approval, and she nodded her okay.

"May 30th it is," Nick said while making his way over to the small table in the back of the room.

"I think it's time for a little schnapps," he said.

Chapter Forty-three

The months passed quickly and May 30, 1953, had arrived. Standing next to her two attendants, her sister, Kati, and her soon to be sister-in-law, Eva, Leni wedded her sweetheart at a wedding Mass at St. Francis Church. Following custom, the guests were invited to a light lunch of soup and *fleisch*. The afternoon was spent visiting or playing cards while the wedded couple fluttered about with the photographer stopping to celebrate with everyone in their path. Following a wedding supper of German goulash and schnitzel, a five-piece band fired up the music and had everyone dancing waltzes, polkas, and tangos.

When the champagne was gone and the crowd beginning to thin, Nick and Theresa looked at each other realizing they had just spent one of the most spectacular evenings of their lives.

"Well, it was a lot different from our little wedding 23 years ago, wasn't it, Theresa?" Nick asked.

"Breathtaking," Theresa said, "from the start to finish."

"This will be the last dance of the evening," the lead singer announced.

Nick led his wife out onto the dance floor.

"Theresa, do you think we gave our girl the

wedding of her dreams?"

"Nick, I think we did *gut*." She smiled up into the eyes of the man she had loved all of her life, resting her head on his shoulder.

"*Ja*, we did *gut*," he repeated.

As the waltzers took their last steps, Nick noticed Leni and Nikolaus bidding their farewells. In the next instant, Nick saw the bridal bouquet whirling in the air, causing shrieks from the young ladies who positioned themselves beneath it. His heart felt heavy and elated at the same time.

When the song ended, Nick and Theresa said goodnight to the last of their guests. Nick looked around the room to find Kati and Jacob departing with Nicky and Rosi.

"Hmm," he said under his breath.

"Nick, what is it?" Theresa asked.

"I wonder what's to become of that situation," he whispered to her. He nodded in the direction of the foursome.

"Well," Theresa said with a smile, "They certainly seem like a good fit, don't they? All four of them."

Theresa slipped her arm through Nick's, resting it in its familiar place. He looked down at her and winked then escorted her out of the hall.

Chapter Forty-four

Leni and Nikolaus moved in with his parents, Maria and Michael, who rented a large enough home to accommodate the newlyweds. In fact, the couple had spent their wedding night and honeymoon on the upper floor, formerly the attic. In 1954, the foursome followed Nick's advice and invested in a duplex on 35th and McKinley, putting an end to renting. In an effort to earn an income on the property, the family occupied the ground floor renting out the upper unit.

It wasn't long until Leni and Nikolaus announced that they were expecting their first baby in March; Nick and Theresa knew that they would be entering one of the happiest times of their lives.

Nick turned and looked at his wife seated next to him in their car. They had a lovely evening with Leni and Nikolaus. Theresa and Leni spent a good part of the evening talking about the new baby coming in March while Nikolaus and Nick debated over their home improvement projects. When Nick noticed Theresa hide a yawn, he had suggested they call it a night.

When they pulled into their driveway, Nick saw Kati and Jacob with Nicky and Rosi sitting on the front porch. Although he had grown used to seeing the foursome together, he began to wonder when they turned their heads to watch Nick park the car.

"*Datee*?" Kati hollered, "can you come over here and talk with us?"

Nick and Theresa walked side-by-side to the front of the house. The sun was setting, casting amber shadows, giving the house a warm glow. Nicky and Jacob stepped forward, their shadows resting upon Rosi and Kati. A thick tension filled the space between Nick and the young men, yet something felt oddly familiar to Nick. When Theresa edged next to him, he reached for her hand and enclosed it within his.

"*Datee*," Nicky began, "we have a unique situation here. All four of us would like to be married," Nicky paused a moment, a grin emerged… "on the same day."

Theresa stepped forward, arms reaching skyward. "A double wedding?" she asked.

"Well, I could see this coming for some time now," Nick said, "but I never suspected a *double* wedding! Whose idea was this?" he asked, a smirk following his question.

"All of us," the group said in unison. They nodded at each other, standing firm.

"We picked July 23rd," Kati said, stepping forward.

"Instead of having two weddings in a row, we can have one big one. It just seems to make the most sense," Nicky added. "Do we have your blessing?"

Nick hesitated for a moment, looking deep into the sparkling blue eyes his son had inherited from him. Facing each other, father and son stood man-to-man while Jacob waited.

"You do!" Nick said with firmness. He stepped closer to shake the hands of the two young men who waited patiently for his approval.

"God has already blessed 1955 for our family," Theresa said, laying her palm on her chest. "Our first grandchild arrives in March and now a double wedding in July! I couldn't be happier. "

Months blended one into another. When Leni delivered a healthy baby boy on March 10, Nick thought he was the happiest he would ever be. Little Alfred visited often and was the light of Nick and Theresa's lives. At the same time, the double wedding plans were moving along nicely and before the family realized it, Kati and Jacob and Nicky and Rosi's special day had arrived.

When Nick opened the door for Theresa and followed her inside St. Michael's Church, he felt the strings tug at his heart once again. He remembered the same feelings at Leni's wedding: elation and sadness at the same time.

As the church filled with family and friends, Nick felt the music surround him as he took notice of the day. Sunlight streamed in through stained-glass windows, its colored rays speckled on the carnations tied to the ends of each pew. Jacob and Nicky stood tall in their crisp, black suits, carnation boutonnieres in place. After nodding toward Nicky, Nick noticed two altar boys moving with grace, lighting altar candles for the ceremony. A church attendant waited in the back corner, readying the runner for the bridal party.

When Theresa left his side to be ushered to her seat, Nick turned on his heels to find his youngest daughter. He headed for the bride's room.

Knocking softly on the door, he turned the doorknob, and stepped into the room. When he saw Kati, she was standing in front of a bank of windows. Her attendants tucked and smoothed the lace and folds of her white, floor-length bridal gown. Nick dropped his head toward his shoulder and smiled. He noticed the sun streaming through her hair, spilling down her narrow shoulders, and knew she was more beautiful than he had ever seen her. When the final touches were made and her veil in place, Nick felt his throat tighten. Swallowing hard, he curled his fingers into his palm and stretched them open, a feeble attempt to relieve the nerves he suddenly felt. He cleared his throat, causing the attention to shift from Kati to himself.

"You look … lovely, Katarina. Jacob is a lucky man."

"Thank you, *Datee*." Kati said.

"Are you ready?" he asked, offering his hand to her. The jitters he had felt just a moment ago vanished when he looked into her eyes. There, he saw the trust she placed in him to help her with this last journey, from *his* daughter to *Jacob's* wife.

Kati nodded. Her excitement was now contagious. Novenka, her maid of honor, gently picked up the bridal bouquet and handed it to her, a spray of white roses and carnations. Kati held out her other hand for her father's steady grasp. Stepping toward her, Nick tucked her arm under his. Walking slowly out of the room, they stepped onto the cloth runner and strolled down the aisle toward Jacob. Rosi and her father proceeded directly behind them.

Chapter Forty-five

A new generation of Nick's family was entering the world. Over the next two years, life moved around a predictable pattern for Nick and Theresa – with the exception of Leni, Kati, and Rosi blessing the family with four more grandchildren. Life was full of an energy Nick and Theresa had all but forgotten.

Theresa fluttered between houses helping out as much as she could. Often times, the little ones came over to *Oma and Ota's*. Life was rich, exciting, and opened up a whole new world. When the grandchildren were over, Nick felt young again, almost playful. Their roles as *Oma* and *Ota* came naturally. Nick never knew such happiness and felt on top of the world until he found himself laid off from his job as a cabinet maker.

It had been less than a month since the layoff, but Nick was struggling. He had never been unemployed in his life. The home they had purchased two years ago on 24th and Galena had sapped much of their income. Although, it was just Nick and Theresa and his parents at home, Nick felt pressure to provide and knew he had to find work and soon.

At night, Nick studied the want ads trying to squeeze his skills into every possible job opportunity until he found something in the newspaper that intrigued him, *For Sale: Liquor Store.*

"You know I spoke with Nicky about buying that liquor store," Nick said to Theresa. Theresa placed the cleaned and dried dinner plates back into the cabinet and turned to face her husband.

"And?" Theresa asked. "What did Nicky say?"

"He's not interested."

"Why not?" Theresa asked. "Rosi said he's tired of working in the cold and wants to get away from butchering."

"He's looking for a dairy farm with his father-in-law and Jacob."

"A what?"

"He wants milking cows."

"*Ja,* I thought I overheard Leni and Nikolaus talking about that last week."

"Why didn't you tell me? I wouldn't have bothered asking him." Nick snapped. He wasn't expecting her to answer him. Ever since the layoff, Nick found himself on edge, his foul mood growing stronger with each day.

"Tell you?" Theresa asked. "You knew as well as I that the three of them go driving around looking at farms to buy. This shouldn't be a surprise to you, Nick."

"I'm going to speak to Nikolaus about it," he said in a matter-of-fact tone.

"Nikolaus?" Theresa asked. She watched Nick scan the want ads most nights, but she had no idea he was considering going into business with Nikolaus.

"*Ja.* He wants to be his own boss just as much as I do. I don't ever want to be laid off from a job again!" Nick yanked at his shirt collar trying to relieve the heat that he felt building inside of him.

Following Theresa to the living room, Nick walked past   his favorite chair but stopped in front of the picture window. Staring into the blackness, Nick's mind was reeling with possibilities. He wanted to use just the right words when speaking to Nikolaus in the morning.

Chapter Forty-six

Nick could hardly wait to drive over to Nikolaus's house in the morning. He knew Leni would be at work and Nikolaus would be watching the two children, Al and Ernie, while recuperating at home from bronchitis. After a quick cup of coffee, he drove the few miles to his house. The two men talked easily about the children, who amused themselves on a blanket on the floor. They discussed Leni's job, and that Nikolaus's parents were doing just fine. When the room fell silent, Nick decided to change the subject.

"You know, Nikolaus," he said, "I've been watching the want ads in the German newspaper and saw that there's a liquor store for sale not too far from here, in a place near Hartford."

"Hartford?" Nikolaus asked.

"It's about 45 miles north of Milwaukee."

"Ah," Nikolaus replied in a flat tone.

"How would you like to take a look at it with me? If it looks good to us, we can work out a partnership?"

Nikolaus popped up onto his elbows from the reclined position he was resting in. Although he was feeling better today, the bronchitis that he had come down with earlier in the week had really left him feeling weak.

"Didn't you have a soda machine back in Calma?"

"*Ja,*" Nick said. "Did Leni tell you that?"

Nikolaus nodded his reply. "She said you made good money at it."

"I did. I know how to sell to people. They like me." Nick said with a grin.

"*Ja,*" Nikolaus said, "I believe that."

"If we do this," Nick explained, "we'll never have to worry about our job security again."

"I can tell you this," Nikolaus added, "I'm real sick of getting bossed around all day by someone else."

Nick looked back at his son-in-law and nodded. That was exactly what he wanted to hear from him.

Nick did not waste any time and called the realty office the next morning about the liquor store he had seen in the newspaper. He was directed to a man by the name of Jim Wagner. Nick grabbed the first available appointment. He and Nikolaus would meet Jim at the liquor store the next morning.

After a fitful night's sleep, Nick and Nikolaus made the trip to Hartford the next morning, met Jim Wagner, and toured the building.

Twenty minutes later, Nick turned to face Nikolaus. "This is not going to work," he said.

"It's too far gone," Nikolaus agreed. "The place must be 200 years old! Look at the old stone walls."

Having overheard the comment, Jim turned to Nikolaus.

"Well, I told your father-in-law on the telephone that the building was a bit rough, but he sounded quite interested."

"Do you have a farm for sale?" Nick interrupted, ignoring Jim's comment. He remembered visiting a broiler farm with Nikolaus just a few weeks ago and was impressed how much money could be made by raising chickens.

"You know, gentlemen," the realtor said. "There is a nice farm for sale not too far from here. It's got about, ohhh," Jim looked up to the sky, rubbing his chin, "I'd say 125 acres that comes with it."

"Where is it?" Nikolaus asked.

"Just outside of the city limits of Hartford. It's in rough shape, but it's going for a fair price."

Nikolaus jabbed Nick in the side, "Remember the broiler farm? We could put up one of those buildings and fill it with chickens, just like my buddy did."

Nick nodded toward his son-in-law, "It's a quick turnaround, a couple of months, and we sell the birds and collect payment."

"Okay, let's take a look at this farm." Nick said.

Nick followed Jim to Hartford farm site. After turning down a dirt road, he gingerly avoided pot holes and good-sized rocks strewn in his path. After getting out of the car, Nick took in a deep breath. He could hardly believe his eyes. He scanned back and forth from the house to the barn. Nikolaus stood behind him saying nothing at all.

The house looked as if it had either survived a tornado or had been abandoned. A cow barn, not far from the house, leaned into the wind, ready to collapse.

"Well, should we take a look at the house first?" Jim didn't wait for a response; instead, he stomped through overgrown grass, blooming thistles, and knee-high weeds.

The two men followed Jim. Each footfall upon the uneven porch steps caused distress to the rusted nails and rotted wood. After a quick knock on the door, Jim proceeded to fit the key into the lock and turned it, allowing them entry into the kitchen.

The first thing that caught Nick's eye was the wood burning stove.

"There's an oil burner in the basement," Jim said after noticing Nick's stare. "But this little baby really heats things up in the kitchen." He patted the wood burner like he would a faithful dog.

Nikolaus closed the door behind him. A rush of air rattled tattered wallpaper above their heads, whipping it to and fro like a kite tail.

Nikolaus spotted a small outhouse standing in the backyard from a nearby window.

"No plumbing," he said in disbelief.

Nick walked over to the kitchen sink. A simple hand pump caught his attention. Out of curiosity, he began working the pump. Squeals of protest followed as he thrust the lever down and up, down and up, but nothing came.

Jim stepped forward, "The man who lives here collects rain water." He signaled outside with his thumb. He stores it in a cistern in the basement."

"Someone actually lives in this place?" Nikolaus wore a look of shock.

"Oh, yes," Jim replied, poker face intact.

"Hard to believe," Nick said. He shook his head from side to side. "How can anyone live in such filth and primitive conditions?"

Jim shrugged but offered no opinion.

When they finished the tour of the house, Nick thought he had seen enough and headed for the car.

"Let's take a look at the cow barn," the realtor suggested and maneuvered the two men across the yard.

Something caught Nick's attention in his peripheral vision. "What is that over there?" he asked.

"Oh, that?" Jim asked. "That's Holy Hill. This property is considered prime real estate because of that shrine." Jim motioned toward the impressive trio of steeples jutting into the sky.

Nick forced himself to appear unimpressed, but the wheels in his head began turning.

Once inside the barn, Nick and Nikolaus drifted off to the side, out of Jim's earshot. They put their heads together while Jim droned on about the available space and potential.

"This barn would have to come down." Nick said.

"*Ja*," Nikolaus agreed. "There's nothing to save here."

"We can put up a three-story building like we saw at the broiler farm," Nick said. "If nothing else, we can sell the property for a profit because of that shrine."

"Are you thinking — we buy the place?" Nikolaus asked.

Nick nodded, lips pressed together.

"How?" Nikolaus asked.

"We sell our houses, but we keep our jobs. That way we have money to remodel."

With a plan in place, the two men turned and walked toward Jim.

Chapter Forty-seven

Over the next couple of weeks, Nick and Nikolaus met with Jim at the Hartford farm site. Theresa and Leni had accompanied them on many of their visits. They walked the land, surveyed the property, discussed and negotiated. When they returned back home, most evenings were consumed in heated discussion about how life would change for everyone if the sale went through. It would mean upheaval moving from Milwaukee, a city they had grown to love, to Hartford, a city they knew nothing about. In the end, after the topic was thoroughly exhausted, Nick looked around the room and into the eyes of his family.

"If we can get it, let's do it," Nick Sr. was the first to share his opinion.

"Maybe if we own something of our own," Nick began, "we can get a piece of this *American Dream* we've heard so much about. Nick stretched both palms up and shook them toward his family.

Theresa nodded but remained silent.

"If I can cross the Atlantic Ocean in a broken-down military ship and survive it, you two should certainly be able to raise some chickens!" Eva burst forth, looking directly at Nick and Nikolaus.

The room was filled with laughter. Nick felt the hand of his father gently slap his back in support. Now, with his family standing behind him, Nick felt ready, ready to take the chance of his lifetime.

After tossing and turning all night, Nick awoke at dawn. Looking down at Theresa, snoring peacefully, he curled over to the side of the bed, dropped his feet as silently as he could onto the wooden floor, and headed out of the room toward the bathroom. The house was quiet, serene. He moved effortlessly making as little noise as possible. This is what he needed: solace, so his mind could clear and his focus sharpen.

After dressing, he headed for the kitchen. He pulled out the canister of coffee grounds, ran the water to fill the pot, and plugged in the percolator. Grabbing a piece of bread, he dropped it into the slot and thrust down the button on the toaster. After gulping down his first cup of coffee between bites of his buttered toast, he headed out the door to pick up Nikolaus. Today was it. It would be the last of their meetings with Jim. They would either come to an agreement and the sale would go through, or they would walk away from an opportunity that might set them apart.

Nick opened the screened door to the kitchen and walked in. Nikolaus followed closely behind him. The room fell silent as Theresa, Leni, and Nick's parents, who were seated at the kitchen table, stopped talking in midstream and looked his way. Nick could feel the suspense hanging in the air like a damp fog.

"Well?" Theresa asked. "Did you get it?"

Nick knew what she was referring to, but he wanted to hold onto the news just a moment longer.

"We got it," he said, stomping his right foot onto the linoleum floor for emphasis. The teacups in the cupboard rattled against one another.

"Ohhh, *Gott in Himmel,*" Eva said. She pressed both of her palms against her chest.

Nick pulled out the empty chair next to Theresa and sat down. Nikolaus took the open seat next to Leni.

"Can we do this, Nick?" Theresa asked. She placed her hand on his forearm.

Nick placed his hand over hers. "I'm not going to lie to you, Theresa. It's going to take a lot of hard work," Nick paused and looked around the table, "from all of us."

"Where do we start?" Eva asked.

"In the kitchen," Nick said, knowing this would please his mother. "We'll use sledge hammers and crow bars and tear down the old walls. It's probably wooden lath and plaster, so removing it will be a dusty, dirty mess."

"Jim Wagner told us the State is buying up properties and tearing them down to build a highway," Nikolaus said.

"41," Nick added. "They are selling the lumber for real cheap — practically giving it away."

"From the torn down houses?" Nick's father asked.

"*Ja,*" Nikolaus said. "We can buy it by the truckload."

Nick's father leaned forward, resting his elbows on the table. "I'll pull out nails and saw up the right lengths."

"That would help," Nick agreed. He rubbed the stubble on his chin.

"I can have my buddy, Morris, help with that too. We'll have to pay him a bit, but it'll be worth it," Nikolaus added.

"Once the old walls are down, we can frame out the new room. We'd like to combine the pantry with the kitchen. We'll make one large room," Nick said. He waved his arms to help explain.

"Then we insulate and hang drywall." Nikolaus continued.

"Where are we going to get the money to buy, to remodel?" Theresa asked.

"We need to sell our houses," Nick said, but he failed to meet Theresa's eyes.

Witnessing the exchange between Nick and Theresa, Nikolaus quickly added, "My parents have agreed to buy us out of our share in the duplex."

"What if our house sells but the remodeling isn't finished? Then what?" Theresa asked. She looked directly at Nick, leaning toward him.

Nick pressed his lips together and inhaled. He looked at Nikolaus.

"You move in with us," Nikolaus said. "My parents have already offered."

"But is there room for us?" Theresa asked, turning her attention to her son-in-law.

"We'll make room."

"That's awfully kind of your parents, Nikolaus," Theresa said.

"Well," Eva said as she slapped the top of her thighs, "who's hungry?" she asked. She sprang to her feet without waiting for a response. Theresa and Leni followed in her path.

Within moments, Nick heard his mother separating the cellophane from the cold cuts. Quick to follow was the knife hitting the cutting board as Leni sliced up cheese and Theresa, sweet onion. A jar of pickled peppers was opened, the pungent aroma filling the kitchen. Nick's mouth watered. The final meeting with Jim had lasted through the lunch hour. Now, several hours later, Nick finally began to relax. He felt famished.

Nick remained silent for a moment, allowing the news to settle. He looked at his hands, folded in front of him. He repeatedly rolled his fingertips across the table, forward then backward. When he looked up, he saw his father smiling at him.

"This could be our chance," his father said. "We could really build something here, something of our very own."

He paused a moment, looking back and forth between Nick and Nikolaus. "What's the plan for the chickens?" he asked.

Chapter Forty-eight

Nick and Nikolaus split the $12,000 price for the farm straight down the middle and formed an equal partnership. Since Nick and Theresa's home sold quickly, they accepted the offer extended to them by Nikolaus's parents and moved into their duplex. There were times when Nick wanted to pull out his hair living in a house full of women, but when he felt at his wits end, he remembered the goal: to finish the renovation and move his family into the farm.

Within the next six weeks, the official real estate closing was over, and Nick and Nikolaus didn't waste any time. They arrived with their picks, hammers, and shovels the following weekend and got started.

Packing up after a long day's work, Nikolaus turned to Nick.

"Since we get slow over the fall and winter at work, I might as well just head out here and keep working all week."

"That would really make a difference," Nick said. Even though Nick had been called back to work, Nick's heart was now tied to the farm, and that's where he really wanted to be.

"We're still pretty busy at the shop," Nick said, "but I'll be here every weekend."

"I can ask a couple of friends who are laid off to come and help me," Nikolaus added.

"*Gut* idea," "Nick said. "Maybe we can get in here by Easter."

Nick cupped his hands behind his head and stretched his legs out in front of him. "I can't believe how far we are on the remodeling," he said to Theresa.

Seated in a nearby chair, Theresa finished the row of stitches she was working on and laid the blanket on her lap. She looked up at Nick. "Well, it certainly helps that Nikolaus is out there working every day."

"Oh! *Ja*" Nick agreed. "He's learned a lot working that construction job. We'll be done with the kitchen by fall."

"Then upstairs?" Theresa asked. "You know how much I want a bathroom up there, Nick."

"Hmm," Nick said. "Well, we have enough to do on the main floor first."

In the end, Theresa got her wish and more: two new bathrooms, one upstairs and one down, along with a newly designed kitchen. They re-insulated walls and installed new windows; the home needed basic plumbing and new electrical as well.

By Easter, just a few months into 1958, Nick moved his family from Milwaukee into the Hartford farm. There were bedrooms for everyone: Nick's parents, Nick and Theresa, and Nikolaus and Leni. Even little Alfred and his brand new baby brother Ernie had a room of their own.

As the months passed, Leni, Theresa, and Eva worked diligently to turn the house into home. They made new curtains, bought new rugs, positioned and repositioned the furniture until everything felt right. The grass was cut, the weeds were pulled, and flowers were planted. A garden was tilled and fertilized. The apple trees were pruned and sprayed. As the dust began to settle with new routines in place, the conversation soon turned toward the future.

Nick's father rose from the supper table and stared out the window. "Are we putting the broilers in the barn?" He shook his head in disgust as he surveyed the collapsing structure.

"No, it'll have to be burned down," Nick said. "It's just too far gone."

"I heard that the Fire Department will do it for a case of beer," Nikolaus said.

The men chuckled and moved into the living room while Leni, Theresa, and Eva began cleaning up the dishes with the children underfoot.

"We need to build a three-story building for the broilers," Nick said. He sat down in his favorite chair.

Nick's father took a seat on the couch next to Nick, and lit his pipe. He paused in between puffs, "Why a three-story?" he asked.

Nikolaus leaned forward. "Do you remember when we took a look at that broiler farm last year?" he asked.

Nick Sr. nodded, giving Nikolaus his full attention.

"Well, that's what they had, so we figured we might as well do the same damn thing."

"Where are you going to get the money?" Nick's father's brow furrowed.

"The bank," Nikolaus said. "I've already been downtown. They said they'd give us a loan."

"Nikolaus also made a deal with that Hungarian in Sussex."

"He told me we can get all the block we want and pay him when we can," Nikolaus said.

"*Gut* job," said Nick Sr. He leaned forward and rested his elbows on the top of his thighs, pipe firmly in his right hand. "How many broilers are we going to be able to fit in the new building?"

"About 12,000," Nikolaus said. They arrive in boxes of 100, and they'll be a day old."

Nick Sr. whistled, rubbing the stubble on his chin.

"That would be 120 boxes?" he asked.

"That's right," Nikolaus said.

"How do we manage 12,000 loose birds?"

Nikolaus stood up from his chair. "They walk around pecking and scratching the floor during the day and roost at night."

"They can feed all day too – we'll install a feeding system using a motorized chain. It'll make one revolution out to the feed hopper every three hours. It'll fill up with corn and then stop once it's made a full circle around the barn." Nick added, swirling his finger in the air above his head.

"Leni and Theresa will keep an eye on the birds, so we can keep our jobs," Nick glanced in Nikolaus's direction, then back to his father. "If the chicks arrive in the spring, we can sell them to the slaughterhouse in summer. And, we don't have to haul them. The slaughterhouse will come here to pick them up."

Nikolaus returned to the recliner and slid into it with ease. "And that's when we make our profit," he said, rubbing his hands together.

Chapter Forty-nine

Nick tapped his shoe against the wall with a repetitiveness that even he was becoming irritated by. He could feel the frustration building inside of him.

"After this, should we try another flock?" he asked Nikolaus. "We ended up even here."

"Well, you're right; I'd thought we'd make more money than we did," Nikolaus said. Lifting his head, he waited for a response from Nick, but was interrupted by the cloud of dust surrounding a fast approaching blue pick-up.

LaVerne Low opened his car door and stepped out of the vehicle. He tucked a thick tablet under his arm and slid a pencil behind his ear. LaVerne was one of Hartford Elevator's top feed salesmen and it was his job to secure incoming orders. Today was one of those days.

Nick had to admit he looked forward to LaVerne's visits. Like Nikolaus, Nick left his job to work full time at the farm. Many days, he felt the loneliness of a day's work without conversation. Although the rewards of building a business were many, it did have its downside.

"Hello, gentlemen," LaVerne said. He walked toward the two men. "I hope I didn't interrupt anything important here. You two look pretty serious."

"No, no, LaVerne." Nikolaus waved his hand to welcome the salesman.

"So, you sold your first flock to the slaughterhouse? How does it feel?" LaVerne asked.

"We did okay; we made out even." Nick said.

"Oh?" LaVerne stepped closer, showing more interest.

"We were hoping to make more money on them," Nikolaus added.

"Why don't you guys put some nests in that building and fill it with laying hens. You'll make $2 a bird."

"$2 a bird?" Nick asked. He looked immediately at Nikolaus, then back to LaVerne.

"That's right," LaVerne said. "That's what all the other egg farmers are ending up with." He moved the tablet from one arm to the other but allowed the pencil to remain behind his right ear.

"How long do they keep a flock?" Nick asked.

"About a year, maybe 18 months." LaVerne said.

"That's a lot longer than broilers," Nick said.

Ignoring Nick's comment for the moment, Nikolaus stepped in closer. "These laying hens," how many eggs do they lay in the 18 months?" he asked LaVerne.

"About an egg a day," LaVerne said, an air of authority grounded his words. "But most of the farmers tell me they get about 300 eggs out of a hen a year."

Nikolaus's eyes shifted. Nick could see his mind was racing with quick calculation. He had been taking care of the checking account, all the bookkeeping, permitting and legal matters for the farm thus far. Nick felt he had knack for the numbers. Besides that, Nikolaus spoke better English, an important asset when dealing with Americans.

"That's 25 dozen eggs a bird," Nikolaus said.

"At 28 cents per dozen," LaVerne grinned but waited for Nikolaus's response.

"Those are good numbers," Nikolaus returned the smile.

"*Ja?*" Nick asked. The numbers jumbled inside of his head. He wasn't use to calculating as quickly as Nikolaus.

"We'd need the rest of this year to get ready, but I think we'd better look into it," Nikolaus confirmed. "We could start 1960 fresh, with laying hens."

"Forget about the broilers," LaVerne agreed. "There's no money in it."

"Appreciate it, LaVerne," Nikolaus said and extended his hand. "I think we're going to wait to place that feed order for now."

"Good idea," LaVerne said and nodded. "Let me know when you're ready to order feed."

Chapter Fifty

The next few years flew by as Nick and Nikolaus transitioned the farm from broilers to layers. Both men could not have been happier with the change in plans.

Now, in 1964, Nick sat back in the wooden chair, shifting his legs to accommodate the accordion that was strapped in place. Thrusting his belly forward, he relieved the stiffness that had been building up in his lower back. He smiled remembering what his father had told him when they boarded the ship to America more than twenty years ago, that one day he would return to visit his sister, Helen. Sure enough, his father was right. While visiting Helen, he bought his new *harmone*, a button-box accordion. It was a totally unexpected purchase for something so dear to his heart which he had missed since his early days in Calma.

The swirling leaves outside caught Nick's attention. He was thankful for the good weather. His family had come together to celebrate his father's 85th birthday. Looking at his father now, Nick recognized the lean on his cane and the snowy white beard he had grown accustomed to seeing. His father was moving slowly now, mingling with his family, but still smiling, still talking, enjoying his life.

Kati and Jacob were the first to arrive with their

five-year-old twins, Heidi and Hertha. Kati was beaming having found out she was pregnant again and due in February. Nicky and Rosi were right behind them. They were anxiously awaiting the arrival of their first child in October.

Nick was overcome with pride remembering the decision the four of them made three years ago, in 1961, when they partnered together and invested in a milking farm near Theresa. It was hard, laborious work but it was an honest living and they felt satisfied. For a long time, Nick had felt saddened that he yearned for his son to become a cabinet maker. But now, years later, the sadness faded with the realization that he felt proud of his son. It was the best decision Nicky had ever made.

And then there was Leni and Nikolaus, who hosted this special day. Nick laughed as he watched their three boys, Al, Ernie, and Frankie, scatter like flies every time they saw their parents heading in their direction while one-year-old Helga held on tight to her mother. Looking at Nikolaus now, Nick was certain the farm would do well under his influence. He was the future and Nick was the past, it was that simple.

Nick straightened up in his chair, repositioning the accordion. He ran his fingers over the front of the instrument, encouraging shrieks and dancing feet from the little ones. He effortlessly punched the buttons, enticing them even more, a wide grin spreading across his face. Musical magic filled the room. Theresa brushed his shoulder and placed a goblet of their homemade wine on a nearby table but as quick as she had arrived, she was off to the next task.

Glancing up to watch the dancers, Nick was

surprised to find his father now standing next to him. He wore a look that Nick hadn't seen in a very long time; an unrushed softness spread across his father's face.

"We made it, Nick," he said. "We really made it." Nick could feel the light pressure of his father's hand resting on his shoulder.

Nick covered his father's hand with his own. "*Ja*, we did," he said and nodded. "For a couple of emigrants, we did okay. What a journey!" Nick's eyes locked with those of his elder's.

"The journey of a lifetime," his father said.

Nick swallowed hard fighting back the unexpected emotion as he watched his father take a seat next to him.

"Happy...Birthday....to...you." All at once a chorus of voices surrounded them. Now huddled together, shoulders touching, their voices gained strength as they continued in song. The small crowd parted allowing Leni and Kati to walk through, holding a two-tiered cake lit with decades of twinkling candles, for the man of honor.

Nick blinked away the surge of emotions forcing his fingers to find their place on the accordion. The instrument's melody filled the room. Leaning his head back, he bellowed, "Happy birthday dear *Datee*, happy birthday to you."

As the evening came to a close and all the partygoers had all gone home, Nick found Theresa puttering away in the kitchen.

"Well, my darling," Nick said, "Is Leni putting the children down?"

"About a half-an-hour ago," Theresa said.

Nick could sense her exhaustion as he watched her lay the towel across the chair to dry.

Are you ready to call it a night?" he asked and seated himself at the table but winced at the stiffness in his knees.

Theresa turned toward him, a smile lighting up her drawn features.

"One day, this will be our birthday party, and we will be 85," Nick snickered.

"*Ja,*" Theresa said. She folded her arms across her chest.

Nick thought he noticed a little something flit across her face.

"And until then?" she asked. "What is to become of us, you and me?"

"Hmmm," Nick paused, "a wise person once told me, we start where we began." Nick waited for her response but was unable to control the grin. "Remember, Theresa?" he asked.

"Ah, yes," Theresa said. "I believe I do remember that conversation."

Their eyes connected, smiling beyond the wrinkled corners, to the younger versions of themselves.

Nick rose to face her, his feet shuffled awkwardly. Without pause, Theresa moved in, closing the gap between them. With hands intertwined, Nick led her from the kitchen to their room, gently closing the door behind them.

Epilogue

In 1967, three years after his 85th birthday, Nick's father died peacefully at home. His wife Eva followed him in death two months later.

Nick and Nikolaus dedicated their lives to the farm. After their first year of raising layers, they increased their flock size from 12,000 to 16,000 to meet demand. In 1964, they found it necessary to build and expand again to accommodate 33,000 hens along with 21,000 pullets. It was during this time, that S & R Egg Farms was born.

In 1976, Nick retired at the age of 65. In his retirement years, he and Theresa wintered in Florida, returning to Wisconsin every spring. In 1999, at the age of 88, he died on St. Valentine's Day, the same age as his father at his death. Theresa struggled during the years that followed Nick's death. Never feeling the same without her partner of 69 years, she followed him in death six years later at the age of 92.

Shortly after Nick retired, Nikolaus sat down with his three sons to decide the future of the farm. Together, they determined expansion was necessary. Nikolaus purchased two farms, one in Waukesha that later evolved into the pullet operation, and the other in Whitewater. As the years progressed, more accounts were acquired and the farm grew. In the 1990s, in an effort to continue the monumental growth, Nikolaus secured Cold Spring Egg Farm, located in Palmyra. The original Hartford farm was sold to a developer in the early 2000s and is now a thriving subdivision with more than 100 homes nestling beneath the Basilica of Holy Hill.

Today, S & R Egg Farms has grown to 2.4 million egg-laying hens, producing approximately two million eggs a day. It employs nearly 200 people and is the largest egg producing farm in Wisconsin. Two of the three farms showcase a large fiberglass chicken on the property to brand their product and help identify their locations.

Nikolaus, now in his eighties, continues to play an integral part in the business. His opinions and advice remain solid, clear, and revered. The farm continues its tradition as a family-owned and managed company spanning three generations.

About the Author

CHRISTINE SCHIMPF has written articles, speeches, poems and student study guides. She earned her Bachelor of Arts degree from the University of Wisconsin and lives with her husband of more than twenty years in Dousman, Wisconsin. More information can be found on her websites: http://www.christineschimpf.webs.com and http://www.nickthejourneyofalifetime.com.

Made in the USA
Charleston, SC
13 June 2012